CHURCH

IN THE STREETS

CHURCH
IN THE STREETS
30 Day Devotional

ROB HILBUN

TATE PUBLISHING
AND ENTERPRISES, LLC

Church in the Streets
Copyright © 2014 by Rob Hilbun. All rights reserved.

This book is designed to provide accurate and authoritative information with regard to the subject matter covered. This information is given with the understanding that neither the author nor Tate Publishing, LLC is engaged in rendering legal, professional advice. Since the details of your situation are fact dependent, you should additionally seek the services of a competent professional.

The opinions expressed by the author are not necessarily those of Tate Publishing, LLC.

Published by Tate Publishing & Enterprises, LLC
127 E. Trade Center Terrace | Mustang, Oklahoma 73064 USA
1.888.361.9473 | www.tatepublishing.com

Tate Publishing is committed to excellence in the publishing industry. The company reflects the philosophy established by the founders, based on Psalm 68:11,
"The Lord gave the word and great was the company of those who published it."

Published in the United States of America

ISBN: 978-1-62902-032-7
1. Religion / General
2. Religion / Christian Life / Devotional
13.12.03

PREFACE

If you greet only your brothers, what more are you doing than others?

Matthew 5:47

"What are we doing that is more?" This is the question that has burdened my heart for some time now. Even the worst of people love those who love them, but what do we do? Are we burdened over the lostness of our neighbor? Do we love people who seem to be unlovable? God calls us to leave our places of comfort, and learn to display love to those who do not know love. He tenders our heart, so we would learn to see the lost people around us. Leonard Ravenhill said, "There are a million roads that led to hell, but not one out." Millions of men and women will forever be totally separated from God in hell. Do we even care? If there is one thing that I've learned while walking with Jesus, it is that if I don't care for Him, I won't care like Him. If I don't talk with Him, I won't talk like Him. If I don't look to Him, I won't look like Him. So the most important thing that I can do on this planet is to meet with Him. Let me say that again in a more personal manner. The most important thing that you can possible do is meet with the One who made you. In doing this we learn to be a light in the midst of a crooked and perverse generation. We learn how to see, talk, act, and live the way God intended. We will be the fork in the road that causes the people on the streets to stop running and begin to seek the Lord. When I refer to "the streets" in this devotion, I am talking about lost people. I'm referring to anyone who does not know Jesus as a friend but an enemy. For whoever, "chooses to be a friend of the world becomes an enemy of God."[1] God is calling us not to a church but as the church. His calling on our life surpasses our natural urge to remain silent in the pews while people are dying in the streets.

His indwelling Spirit constantly reminds us that He is alive and active. The righteousness of God is not stationary, so His children should also be righteous wherever they go. If God is holy in heaven, He is also holy here on earth. If God were only holy in heaven, what a terrible state we would find ourselves in, here on earth. God is holy at all times and at all places. The same should be true for the church body. If we are to be the church God is calling and forming us to be, we must be the Church in the streets as well as in the pews.

This daily devotion is a modest attempt to help aid God's children to appear as a light in the midst of a crooked and perverse generation.[2] Each day is designed to focus on a different aspect of evangelism in our Christian walk.

DEPENDENT ON HIS SPIRIT
PART I

"Blessed are the poor in spirit"

Matthew 5:3

God can use the man who walks around town with his chest puffed out, preaching of his own self-righteousness. He can use the prideful teenager who sings on stage like he has earned his gift. He can even use the lady who considers herself holy because she is not near as bad as her neighbor. But these people cannot expect to be used much. Jesus said, "Blessed are the poor in spirit"[3]. He did not say, "Blessed are the arrogant in spirit". God chooses to bless people who are spiritually bankrupt. His blessing falls on the man who understands he has nothing to offer spiritually apart from what the Lord has given. "Every element of self-reliance must be slain by the power of God. Complete weakness and dependence will always be the occasion for the Spirit of God to manifest His power."[4] If we desire to be used by Him we must completely rely on his Spiritual leadership. Our natural devotion to the Lord will always lead to sin, this is why we must allow His Spirit fuel our devotion. Once we begin to think we have something to bring to the table, we take God out of the role of King and Lord of our life, and replace Him with our own kings and lords. Just as the Israelites pleaded with Samuel to give them a king, we begin to choose our own way over His. They rejected God as their King and wanted to look to a man to lead them. Who is more righteous than God? Who can match His majesty? Who are His counselor's? Who gives Him wisdom and discernment? Why do we not allow Him to reign alone? We should never say, "I can do this on my own." But instead let us always say, "You are my Lord; I have no good apart from you."[5] This should be the plea of our heart. "I have nothing! But I am yours!"

POOR IN SPIRIT— BREAKING THE BONDAGE OF SIN

"The Spirit helps us in our weakness"

Romans 8:26

We did not earn salvation nor can we earn sanctification. They are both the work of God. We can, however, quench the Holy Spirit during sanctification. We can stand in the way of what the Lord wants to do in our life. The good news is that He will perfect what He has started within us,[6] but let us not stand in the way of His workings. We must allow God to root out every deep dark sin that keeps us from being the church we are called to be. This is what A. W. Tozer says concerning rooting out those dark sins, "…he should remember that this is holy business. No careless or casual dealings will suffice. Let him come to God fully determined to be heard. Let him insist that God accept his all, that he take things out of his heart and himself reign there in power." Breaking the bondage of sin takes His strength not ours. We, however, must have a genuine heart of submission. The answer lies in whom or what we are submitting to? If we continue to submit to our pleasures and other idols then God will never reign supreme in our life. Let us say again to the Lord, "I have nothing! But I am Yours!"

When I was younger I always looked forward to staying with my grandparents during the summer. I would join my brother, sister, and cousins as we stayed on the farm. Every day was a different kind of battle. Only one thing stayed the same: BOYS VS. GIRLS. I would spend hours catching little green tree frogs. They were not scary, poisonous, or even big but they put fear in all the girls. This was one of my favorite weapons. It was built around a lie. The lie was that these little slimy frogs could do much harm to every girl on the planet. For some reason my sister believed it. Those little frogs would get her to use every ounce of her being. She would run, jump, or even cry at the sight of a little frog. Everyone knew that a frog had no power over her except what she gave it. "Freedom from spiritual conflicts and bondage is not a power encounter; it's a truth encounter."[7] Satan and the other devils are like those little frogs: deceiving people into fearing them more than God. Their power is in the lie. Satan is the father of lies[8] who deceives the whole world[9], and consequently the whole world is under the influence of the evil one.[10]" Jesus said, "You shall know the truth, and the truth shall make you free."[11] All my sister had to do is grab that frog and throw it and it would never bother her again. If we want to escape the bondage of sin we must realize that Christ has already done the work; all we have to do is believe it.

Seek the Lord as you read and study 2 Timothy 2:20-26.

Make This Your Prayer Today

It was you Lord that saved me
It was you Lord that changed me
It is you Lord that saves alone
I have nothing! But I am yours!
Please give me wisdom and discernment Lord
Allow me to share the good news today
Make me bold, urgent, and compassionate
In the name of Jesus I pray,

Amen.

"…let your adorning be the hidden person of the heart with the imperishable beauty of a gentle and quiet spirit, which in God's sight is very precious."

1 Peter 3:4

SPIRITUAL LAZINESS

"… He did with all His Heart, and Prospered."

2 Chronicles 31:21

The sluggard wakes up and goes outside. He expects to see a great harvest yet there is nothing but wasteland. He should have *considered the ways of the ant* but he didn't.[12] He spent his days and nights sleeping. Even when his eyes were open he was daydreaming of what could be. He told his friends and family of his great plans but never sought council from the Lord. He would often think to himself, "I am going to be mighty for the Lord" but he never put forth effort to meet with Him. He lived off of the scraps of others as they taught in the squares and courtyards. He thought, "I can do better than them, if I only had the opportunity." But it wasn't the lack of opportunity that was holding him back. He was too blinded by his own careless pursuits and vain attempts of quick fame. He wanted an overnight harvest. He should have known that, "God does not give harvest to lazy men except harvest of thistles, nor is He pleased to send wealth to those who will not dig in the field to find it's hidden treasure."[13]

Work! This is why we are here. This is not a vacation. There is a reason that the Lord chose to work six days and rest one. There is work to be done. There are souls to be won. Let us lift up our eyes; the harvest is ripe and ready for picking.

> *"The soul of the sluggard craves and gets nothing, while the soul of the diligent is richly supplied."*
>
> *Proverbs 13:4*

I can still hear my parents telling me, "Go outside." As a child I was not allowed to spend a large amount of time sitting inside playing video games or watching TV. I had to find something to do outside. Many of those days I spent with my brother making trails for my four-wheeler to go through. I remember the first tree I cut down with my machete. Three weeks, four blisters, and a nice knot on my head later—the tree came tumbling down. I cannot even begin to explain my excitement as I watched the tree fall to the ground. I can also remember the first person that I shared Christ with. He was a lot like that tree. He was as tough as nails. He was trying to give up a smoking habit that he picked up when he was ten. I worked and worked on him for weeks. There were times when I wanted to give up but I knew the labor was not in vain. I never felt like I was chopping alone for God chops *"down the tall cedars"*[14]. His Spirit led as I opened my mouth. I chopped where He told me to and He cut down the sinful teenager until he was right where He wanted him, broken enough to realize that he was in need of a Savior. This harvest in my life only took place because of diligence. The man who is diligent will receive all that his spirit and flesh need, but the sluggard will always be wanting but will never attain. Laziness!!! This is a great problem. There is laziness in the pulpits, in the Sunday School classes, in the small groups, in the homes, at the workplace, in the schools, and in the streets. Lazy kids are being taught by lazy parents. Lazy church members are being taught by lazy pastors. How can we ever expect to see a great harvest if we don't work. If the nurse wants to see her fellow nurses come to know Jesus then she must witness. If the fireman wants to see his fellow laborers talk of the Lord let him preach of the fire to come. We are watchmen let us do our job. It's time to wake up and get to work.

Are you allowing too much time to slip away when the Lord is calling you to action?

Has God given you a great desire but you haven't even begun to work towards it?

Seek the Lord as you read and study James 2:14-26.

Wake Up and *Make This Your Prayer Today*

God I don't want to be lazy
I want to serve you with all of my heart
I know I have been sent here for a reason
Give me strength to act on your calling

Your presence is so much better than my possessions
Please give me wisdom and discernment Lord
Allow me to share the good news today
Make me bold, urgent, and compassionate
In the name of Jesus I pray,

Amen.

"Go to the ant, O sluggard; consider her ways, and be wise."

Proverbs 6:6

THE PRAYING LIFE
PART I

> *"The effective prayer of a righteous man can accomplish much."*
>
> *James 5:16* NASB

We must start with prayer. We often say our prayers, but do we ever pray? An old sage spoke of prayer as thinking God's thoughts after him. True Spirit-led prayer is God putting his burden into and through our heart. One way we know that we have a fruitful prayer life is by inspecting our burdens. Are they God-driven? Does His Word fuel them? "By a strange paradox those who pray most, feel they pray little. This much is sure: No one who prays, struts!"[15] True prayer must be offered in humility. Christian, our theology teaches us that God is able to act, but do we believe He will? When we pray, "God, wake us up!" Do we believe that He will answer our prayer? It is easy to say that God can move mountains but do we believe that He will? Knowing that God is able to do something does not take much faith, but believing that God will do something takes great faith. The summer of 2013, some students and myself were sharing Christ with some homeless people in the Tampa Bay area. We walked up to a man and a woman who were on the street smoking weed. We gave them some water and began to share with them. The lady said she was in need of thirty-five cents. We didn't have any money on us. We asked her what she needed it for. She said she needed a bus ticket. I began to tell her that God could provide a way for her to travel if she believed. I asked her if she believed that God could provide a bus ticket for her. She replied, "Oh yes, He can." So I asked her if we could pray that God would make a way for her to get to where she needed to go. She said, "Of course." As soon as we bowed our heads to pray, a man came up to us and said, "Hey, I got an extra bus ticket. Does anyone need it?" The woman was amazed and began to shout, "I just witnessed a miracle! I just witnessed a miracle!" The man sitting next to the woman put down his weed and said, "You guys can pray for me too." It's awesome how God knows what we need before we even ask. Today, let us step back and take a look at our prayer life.

PRAYERLESSNESS

"…God forbid that I should sin against the LORD *in ceasing to pray for you"*

*1 Samuel 12:23 (*KJV*)*

In my ministry, I've seen hundreds come to know Jesus, with few hours of prayer each week. It breaks my heart now to think of how many hundreds were lost because of my lack of prayer. I can't imagine what would have taken place over the last ten years, if I had sought the Lord more diligently in prayer. A. W. Tozer said, "We are not only going to be judged for what we have done; we are going to be judged for what we could have done."

We either love or hate prayer. There is not much room for middle ground since it is a heavy work. "Those who pray love to pray."[16] Only those who pray understand man's potential in the hands of the Almighty. The prayer of a man will be his sword of victory. On the other hand, the lack of prayer will be his sword of demise. Robert Murray McCheyne used to say, "Prayer is a fearful weapon in the hands of a holy God." The amount of time we spend in prayer can either be pleasing or disgusting. In 1 Samuel, God treats our lack of prayer as a sin. "God forbid that I should sin against the Lord in ceasing to pray…" We may spend hours watching movies or playing at the ballpark, but if we are not prayed up we are doing nothing but wasting time. We must seek the Lord in prayer about all aspects of our life. The Lord eagerly waits for our conversation, like a parent waits to see their child after a couple of days of absence. A consistent prayer life produces consistent spiritual growth. On the other hand, an inconsistent prayer life produces inconsistent spiritual growth. Too often, we pray to God if we are not too tired; we go meet with others in prayer, if we don't have anything better to do; we will spend time in prayer, if we haven't filled our hour. I long for the day when I go to the prayer room and I have to wait outside because it is occupied. Oh to pray with others outside because the prayer room is too full. Maybe then our prayers will be answered in the streets.

A few summers back, I got the opportunity to take our youth group to Convisa, Guatemala. I was walking with some teenagers through the village and we saw eight men working with pipes, trying to get water to their village. I told them we wanted to pray for them, as they worked. I asked them specifically what I could pray for them about. They told me to pray to the One who can make it rain. I assured them only the one true God can cause it to rain. I told them that for three and a half years God kept the rain from the Israelites, and God heard the prayer of one man named Elijah. For the effective prayer of a righteous man can accomplish much. I prayed out loud for the men. I prayed that God would open the floodgates. A few hours later, during a worship service, it began to storm. It rained for the next two days. I went back to those men because I wanted to share the gospel with them. Before I could speak a word, my translator spoke boldly to the men and said, "Do you have something to say?" And they replied, "Yes, you prayed for rain and it rained." I told them that God hears the prayers of his people.

Wonders will happen if we are a praying people. God is calling us to be holy men and women of prayer. May our hearts be broken over the lostness of men. The American Church prayer life has been dry for far too long. Are we Christians playing in the yard, while men perish? This go-to-church-once-a-week-and-pay-your-tithes-and-sing-in-the-choir Christianity is a sham, if that is the limit of our Christian service and the extent of our passion for souls.[17] Let us pray. Let us learn to pray. We will never be the Church in the streets if we don't pray. If we don't pray we won't care.

Seek the Lord as you read and study 1 Samuel 1.

Make This Your Prayer Today

Lord, Teach me to be a man/woman of prayer
Break my heart for the things that break yours
Teach me what it truly means to serve you
I love you
I am nothing without you
Give me strength to continue to work through prayer
Please give me wisdom and discernment Lord
Allow me to share the good news today
Make me bold, urgent, and compassionate
In the name of Jesus I pray

Amen

A couple of the men who asked for rain

"You prayed for rain and it rained."

"In whom we have boldness and confident access through faith in Him."

Ephesians 2:18

OBEDIENT IN THE SMALL THINGS

"We come into God's house and say, "The Lord is in his holy temple, let us all kneel before Him." Very nice. I think it's nice to start a service that way once in a while. But when any of you enter your office on Monday morning at nine o'clock, if you can't walk into that office and say, "The Lord is in my office, let all the world be silent before Him," then you are not worshiping the Lord on Sunday. If you can't worship Him on Monday you didn't worship him on Sunday. If you don't worship Him on Saturday, you are not in very good shape to worship Him on Sunday."[18]

"She tied the scarlet cord in the window"

Joshua 2:21

Obedience in the small areas of our life may not lead thousands to Christ, but it will help us stay above reproach so we can be a pure witness. Christian, do not think for a moment that God will not care if you do not return your shopping cart to its proper place. As Christians, we must always been on guard. Rahab was given a small task but it had life or death consequences. All she had to do was tie a scarlet cord on her window and she would be saved. Are you being obedient in the small things? Have you observed the two ordinances of believers' baptism and the Lord's Supper? To neglect these is to display the unloving disobedience in your heart. From now on, be blameless in everything, even the tying of a thread, if that is what's commanded. Jericho's walls fell flat: Rahab's house was on the wall, and yet it stood undisturbed. Have you tied the scarlet cord, with an intricate knot in your window, so that your trust can never be removed?[19]

"But if you carefully obey his voice and do all that I say, then I will be an enemy to your enemies and an adversary to your adversaries."[20]

Far too often, we only hear what we want to hear. Children are told that if they clean their room and make it spotless, they can go outside to play. It seems like every time I was told that, as a child, I would forget the spotless part. I would rush to finish, not really caring about the cleanliness of the room. I did just enough to get by. Leonard Ravenhill tells a story in his book *Revival Praying* that reminds me of paying special attention to the Spirit as He speaks.

John Greenleaf Whittier stood in speechless wonder gazing at Niagara Falls. He marveled at the milky cataract, as it hurled itself down into the canyon below, and was amazed at the thunder of its waters. But he was yet more astonished when an Indian plucked his sleeve and said, "An enemy is coming!" "How do you know?" asked Whittier. "Because," replied the warrior, "I heard a twig break." John Whittier had heard nothing but the thundering of the waters, yet the sensitive ears of the alert hunter had heard the snapping of a twig above the roar of those raging waters. If we are going to be obedient in the small things we must be alert to his speaking. What is he saying today? Is he telling you to cut your neighbor's grass? Is he pleading you to come and meet? Is he commissioning you to go? Listen carefully to the sound of twig breaking. Though there maybe rushing rivers of technology all around; listen to his voice. The Lord may be trying to speak to you like He did the prophet Elijah, "And he said, "Go out and stand on the mount before the LORD." And behold, the LORD passed by, and a great and strong wind tore the mountains and broke in pieces the rocks before the LORD, but the LORD was not in the wind. And after the wind an earthquake, but the LORD was not in the earthquake. And after the earthquake a fire, but the LORD was not in the fire. And after the fire the sound of a low whisper."[21]

Seek the Lord as you read and study Numbers 20:7-12.

Make This Your Prayer Today

Lord teach me to pay special attention to your words
Even though the world is rushing around me
Let me hear your callings
I want to be obedient in the small things as well as the large

Please give me wisdom and discernment Lord
Allow me to share the good news today
Make me bold, urgent, and compassionate
In the name of Jesus I pray,

Amen.

"You are my friends if you do what I command you."

John 15:14

THE PURSUIT:

PART I

"God is spirit, and those who worship Him must worship in spirit and truth."

John 4:24

WORSHIPERS THEN WORKERS

No one can worship God in spirit and in truth for very long and not feel obligation to His holy service. God's calling is far too strong to resist. "Fellowship with God leads straight to obedience and good works."[22] This is the way that the Lord leads us, but woe to us, if we turn to the right or to the left without worshiping him first. Worship must come first before work and not vice versa. Out of a blazing fellowship with the Lord comes a zeal to his holy callings. The only acceptable workers for the Lord are those who have learned the lost art of worship. His goal is to turn rebels into worshipers; and this will also become our goal for the people in the streets as we meet with him. If we are to know the Lord well, we must constantly have Him on our heart and mind. Anything that keeps us from our personal time with the Lord is our enemy, however harmless it may appear to be. We must be careful not to allow things to steal our attention away from Jesus causing harm to our souls.

WORSHIP IN SPIRIT

The Holy Spirit truly knows how to worship in an acceptable manner. If the Holy Spirit is not a part of our worship, then we are not worshiping rightly. In many churches today, we teach our people to worship how they please, but if worship is left up to them, they will fall short every time. We cannot worship as we please. If we choose our own way, we will choose in our flesh instead of worshiping in spirit. Our spirit is in constant opposition to our flesh, which is corrupt. The Holy Spirit must lead us into the throne room. We cannot make it on our own. When we worship in our own way, we quench the Spirit and tell the Lord that we know how to worship him best. In actuality, we can't even pray right without the help of his Spirit.[23] "Worship originates with God and comes back to us and is reflected from us, as a mirror. God accepts no other kind of worship."[24] We must learn to have encounters with the Lord until, like Moses, we have a glow about us.

WORSHIP IN TRUTH

We have a shocking amount of nature worshipers nowadays. They twirl around in fields and call every sound a melody, every plant beauty, and every word they write in their journal is poetry. We must be careful not to mistake a feeling of worship for true godly worship. "Some people admire everything, some admire nothing and some admire the wrong things, but God has given us Himself and says, 'Here, admire Me, I am God.'"[25] We have filled our services with lights, humor, performers, social clubs, coffee shops, fitness centers, bookstores, warm greetings, and zealous spirits; but hardly anywhere do we find a gathering marked by the overshadowing presence of God. God seeks people who worship in truth. If we do not worship with a sincere heart; we must forget all the other gadgets, attractions, and evangelism tools; and learn to be real before God. We cannot worship God rightly with cloudy vision, or with a double-minded nature. We must strip down before the Lord and say, "I can do nothing on my own for I am a sinner saved by your grace."[26]

Are you worshiping the Lord in spirit and truth? Will you let your worship fuel his holy calling on your life today?

Seek the Lord as you read and study John 4.

Make This Your Prayer Today

Jesus, teach me to worship you rightly
I pray that my worship will fuel my work for you

Lord keep me away from anything false
I want to be real before you
I need help worshiping you
Please give me wisdom and discernment
Allow me to share the good news today
Make me bold, urgent, and compassionate
In the name of Jesus I pray,

Amen.

"Whoever drinks the water I give them will never thirst. Indeed, the water I give them will become in them a spring of water welling up to eternal life."

John 4:14

THE PRAYING LIFE
PART II

"I have drunk neither wine nor strong drink, but I have been pouring out my soul before the Lord."

1 Samuel 1:15

Praying people are not lazy. Prayer takes work. The ineffective prayer is thrown up in the air with no care if it is received or not. These prayers are more of a tradition than plea, carelessly spoken before meals and before we sleep. Not only are these prayers ineffective, but they are also a terrible witness to the people around us. If we go and fight with no armor, swords, unction, or authority; what's stopping the young converts from doing the same? If they hear these careless words we say without concern, they will offer up the same kind of prayers. If we are not pursuing the heart of God in effective prayer, we are leading our disciples further and further away from the Lord. There is an old story told of Arthur Rubinstein (a

Polish- American classical pianist) that often reminds me of prayer. The maestro said, "If I miss my piano practice one day, I know it; if I miss practicing two days, my friends know it; if I miss these exercises three days, the world knows it." The same should be true of us, if we are a praying people.

THE QUICKLY ANSWERED PRAYER

And this is the confidence that we have toward him, that if we ask anything according to His will He hears us.

1 John 5:14

Broken over my sin as a nine-year-old boy, I pleaded with the Lord to take this load off of me. I was on my bed crying out, and the moment the words reached my tongue, I felt instant relief. My soul wasn't troubled anymore. My chains were broken, and I experienced true peace for the first time in my life. God was not slow to answer this prayer. He was eagerly waiting the moment that I would call out His name. When He sees that we are in instant need, He makes sure that we are answered quickly. Jesus said, "*What father among you, if His son asks for a fish, will instead of a fish give him a serpent;*"[27] If we are in need of a fish then He will give us a fish.

THE LINGERING PRAYER

"I called Him, but he gave no answer."

Song of Solomon 5:6

"The Lord, when He has given great faith, has been known to test it by long delays. He has allowed His servants' voices to echo in their ears as if the heavens were brass."[28] Every morning, as I get ready for the day, I listen to the same worship songs. I play the same songs because the music reminds me of special times in my life with God. They help me get prepared for my morning devotion with the Lord. Sometimes the Lord desires to hear the same songs over and over again from His children. These prayers may test the commitment of the believer, but it is also a beautiful song to the Lord. "Prayer is another way of telling God that we have all confidence in Him, but no confidence in our own native powers."[29] Neglect of prayer is just like we are saying that we don't need the Lord's help. Will we continue to seek the Lord in intercession even when we don't feel Him? Do we care enough about our cause that we would be on our face day after day to hear His voice? This is the work of prayer. Though it is a tough work, it is well worth fighting for. "It is the hard-working farmer who ought to have the first share of the crops."[30] The farmer shouldn't receive a dime, if he doesn't work. If we are careless in our dealings, we will not hear a word from the Lord. One thing is true: we can't expect to bear much fruit if we are not doing the work of prayer.

"Where there are no oxen, the manger is clean, but abundant crops come by the strength of the ox."[31]

Before the use of tractors, it was impossible for men to see a great harvest without the work of the ox, or donkey, etc. Though, the oxen brought abundant crops, it took a lot of work to keep the manger clean. Christian, we must do the work of prayer if we want to see people saved. It does take a lot of work, but it is a commendable work.

Do you have a desire to see people saved? Do you care enough for your friends, family, and enemies to pray for them? Even if takes work?

Prayer fuels true evangelism. If we are not a praying people, we are not a saving people. If we are not a praying people, we are a lazy people.

Seek the Lord as you read and study James 5:13-20.

Make This Your Prayer Today

Thank you Lord for hearing my prayers
Lord teach me what I should pray
Give me strength to continue to work through prayer
Please give me wisdom and discernment Lord
Allow me to share the Good News today
Make me bold, urgent, and compassionate
In the name of Jesus I pray

Amen

"But Peter put them all outside, and knelt down and prayed; and turning to the body he said, "Tabitha, arise." And she opened her eyes, and when she saw Peter she sat up."

Acts 9:40

SERVE THE LORD
WITH GLADNESS

"Serve the Lord with gladness…"

Psalm 100:2a

Why would anyone want to come to Jesus, if they see us serving him with such drudgery? Instead of teaching the world that there is freedom in Christ, our actions often speak of chains. The chains of the ungrateful man will lead the world to think our belief in Christ Jesus does nothing but enslave us. "Those who serve God with a sad countenance, because they do what is unpleasant to them, are not serving him at all: they bring the *form* of loyalty, but *life* is absent."[32] The moment our service becomes a "chore or a must do", instead of a "joy and get to"; we must stop and seek the Lord. If we attempt our duties without delighting in the Lord, we invite sin to join us while we work. We must *first* understand that we cannot serve the Lord with gladness, unless we are satisfied with the Lord in all areas of our life. It is easy to be glad in areas that are recognized by the world as a thing of honor, but how can we scrub a bathroom floor with the same gladness. We must be totally satisfied with Him. The apostle Paul said, "I count everything as loss because of the surpassing worth of knowing Christ Jesus my Lord."[33] When we can do away with the worldly concerns, everything and anything we do can be done with great delight.

I despised roofing houses with every ounce of my being. My brother would drag me away with him, in the early mornings, during my summer vacations while I was in high school. I can still feel the fiberglass in my arms and legs. Serving the Lord with gladness was the last thing on my mind. I would much rather serve the Lord in my bed. The last summer that I worked with my brother, God was also doing a work within us. We both really began to seek the Lord. Our conversations changed over time. We used to talk of baseball or whatever came to our mind, but the Lord was becoming our joy. He quickly became the topic of our conversations. I will never forget my seventeenth birthday. I would have to say, it has made my top three favorite birthdays. I sat on my grandmother's roof watching the sunrise with my brother, while roofing her house. We talked of our favorite conversation, Jesus. He was our heart, so He was all we wanted to talk about. I thought to myself, "I cannot think of another place I would rather be but here roofing this house." A duty that used to be drudgery to me became an act of praise just by being satisfied with the Lord. If we can be satisfied with

CHURCH IN THE STREETS

Jesus alone, we will be able to serve the Lord with gladness in all areas of your life. No matter if you are a stay at home mom consumed with raising the little ones, or a single college student with few concerns.

> *"He was anointed with the oil of gladness beyond your companions."*
>
> *Psalm 45:7*

We as the church have a well full of joy that is never-ending. Look at the Lord Jesus who had songs of gladness even in the deepest darkest of times, even when He was beaten and earthly happiness had gone. Let us imagine the gladness of our Savior, when He was a teenager. It must have been such a joy to labor beside Him as a carpenter, the True Servant who never complained and always seemed to enjoy His work. Even if we came to work in a bad mood or discouraged He would lift our spirits, He would speak life into us. Let us take His perfect example. "There is a river whose streams make glad the city of God."[34] We must be aware, alert, awake, attentive, responsive, and sensitive to the Spirit if we are going to serve Him with gladness. Let us keep Jesus in our conversations and continue to drink from the streams of joy that God offers only to His children.

Are you serving the Lord with gladness?

Are there areas in your life that you need to give to the Lord and rejoice in?

For further study read Romans 5

Make This Your Prayer Today

Lord I am satisfied with You
You give me Joy even in the darkest of times
I pray that I would labor with gladness
I pray I would be an encouragement to all who see
When they ask I will tell them of the reason I sing
It is You and You alone
Please give me wisdom and discernment Lord
Allow me to share the Good News today
Make me bold, urgent, and compassionate
In the name of Jesus I pray,

Amen.

"…my heart is glad, and my whole being rejoices"

Psalm 16:9

DO YOU LOVE THEM?

"The second is this:
'You shall love your neighbor as yourself.'
There is no other commandment greater than these."

Mark 12:31

As our love for the Lord grows so does our love for people. This is one reason why "love your neighbor" is the second command and not first. Loving God fuels our love for people. It's easy to make promises but strength comes from performance. So let us not just talk of love but let us display it to the people in the streets.

As a young minister, I grew out my facial hair and changed my appearance, so I could look as old as possible. I thought that I must look older if people were going to listen. When it came time to preach, I was amazed at how attentive they were. Now as I look back, I know it was not because of my appearance or preaching ability that they listened, but because of God's grace and the love He gave me for them. I truly cared, so they listened. If the people in the streets know that we care, they will listen.

LOVING THE UNLOVABLE

"Whoever mocks the poor insults his Maker; he who is glad at calamity will not go unpunished."[35] Some people are very hard to love. They seem to almost be unlovable, but this is by no means the truth. Most of the time the barrier between us is rooted out of pride. Who are we to think that we are better than another? It will be good for us to remember that God will not dwell in hateful thoughts, polluted thoughts, destructive thoughts, covetous thoughts, or prideful thoughts.

Maybe the way they speak or act aggravate us? Maybe the way they dress or look appall us? But how does the Lord see them? If we make fun of them, we are insulting their Maker. If we have been shrewd in finding out the defects in others, remember that will be exactly the measure given to us.[36] We must learn to treat their soul with greater importance than their appearance or actions. Their soul should mean much more to us than their annoying traits or words. When we are concerned over lost souls we will have the deepest and weighty thoughts. So, we must not deal carelessly when the salvation of man is at stake. We must learn to look past their imperfections, if we are to win them for Christ. I am not saying we shouldn't show them their sin, for repentance must come if they are to be saved. I am simply saying, we must love them as God loves them. God sees us through the precious blood of Jesus so let us remember, when we boast, our boasting can only be in the cross. Let us remember that when He enters a life that life is eternally altered.

When I was in ninth grade there was a new kid who started coming to our youth group. For some reason he really got on my nerves. At first it wasn't that bad, but over the next couple of years I built up such hatred towards him. I often thought, "Why is this kid so aggravating?" Every time I saw him, I just wanted to beat him up, and I accomplished that goal pretty often. Over the years, the Lord began to show me that he was not the problem but I was. I allowed sin towards him block the way the Lord wanted me to see him. God showed me that he loves him deeply, and I should love him as well. It was tough, but I confessed my sins to the Lord and to the kid. At that very moment, the Lord built a bond between us that I can't explain. I learned that we cannot pray in love and live in hate and still think we are worshiping God.[37]

Is there someone that the Lord is dealing with you about today? Are you allowing their appearance or actions to stand in the way of you showing them the love of Jesus? Maybe you need to repent and seek the Lord's wisdom.

Seek the Lord as you read and study 1 Corinthians 13.

Make This Your Prayer Today

Lord I want to care for people
I want to care for their soul more than the way they look or act

Help me to see people the way you do
May others look at me and give glory to you
Please give me wisdom and discernment Lord
Allow me to share the good news today
Make me bold, urgent, and compassionate
In the name of Jesus I pray,

Amen

"When he saw the crowds, he had compassion for them,
because they were harassed and helpless, like sheep
without a shepherd."

Matthew 9:3

LEARNING HOW TO DIE

"Let us also go, that we may die with Him."

John 11:16

During our pursuit of the Lord we must learn to die. *Jesus said to his disciples, "Whoever wants to be my disciple must deny themselves and take up their cross and follow Me."*[38] We may have heard this passage preached more times than we can remember but let us look at this verse like we did the first time we heard it. It is still true. It is still tough. It is still a command. We *must* deny ourselves. "We know that our old self was crucified with Him in order that the body of sin might be brought to nothing…"[39] We must learn to consider all things as rubbish, in order to gain Christ.[40] Christian, you will never care about others, if you are too consumed by your own desires. How often do you listen to the Holy Spirit as He leads you to share the good news? How often do you answer the call to get off the couch and get to work? Do you hear His voice as he bids you to come? Sit with Him so you can learn to die like Him.

> *"Truly, truly, I say to you, unless a grain of wheat falls into the earth and dies, it remains alone; but if it dies, it bears much fruit."*
>
> John 12:24

Jan Overstreet, a town legend dying of cancer, raises her fist in the air on her deathbed and says, "Devil, I'm going to sting you," as she hears the passage of the scripture, *oh death where is your sting41* read over her. The life Mrs. Jan lived, no doubt in my mind, made the Devil angry. Few modern Christians die with such dignity and Christ-centered perspective. In fact, one might regard Overstreet's death a glorious one, a death that brought much fruit. As hundreds filled her house on the last days of her life, she proclaimed the good news and pleaded with sinful people to repent while there was still time.

Mrs. Overstreet's physical death provides a great example of how we should live. We must die to our sinful nature, so there can be much fruit spiritually. We must learn to live as Jesus did. In humility, he counted others more significant than himself.[42] As our view of God gets bigger, we begin to walk more and more humbly. Jesus said, "Learn of me; for I am meek and lowly in heart."[43] Humility must come first, if we are seeking holiness. Jesus teaches us not only to look out for our *own interests, but also to the interests of others*[44]. He *made himself nothing*, even though from him precedes everything, including all good things. John the Baptist said, *"He must increase, but I must decrease."*[45] The apostle Paul said, *"Indeed, I count everything as loss because of the surpassing worth of knowing Christ Jesus my Lord"*[46]. He went on to say, *"I die every day!"*[47]

Sadly, many church-goers today have chosen possessions over God's presence. But if the Church is going to be what it was called to be, its members must learn to deny themselves. We must consider our possessions as rubbish compared to His presence. The more that we delight in His Word and feast on His grace, the more insignificant the things of this world appear. The higher we escape on the mountain of God, the smaller our houses and toys look. Let us see to it that every thing, every place, and every hour is given to the Lord in worship.

"And if your right hand causes you to sin, cut it off and throw it away. For it is better that you lose one of your members than that your whole body go into hell."[48]

Our "right hand" is the best thing we have. I use my right hand to do most things throughout the day—from turning off my alarm clock in the morning to brushing my teeth at night before I sleep. Lucifer's right hand was his beauty, but he allowed his right hand to stand in the way of worship, so he was cut off from the presence of God. Abraham's right hand was Isaac, and God tested him to see if he would cut it off. God wanted to see if Abraham loved his right hand more than he loved God. What is your right hand? Have you put it ahead of the Lord? Maybe it's your job or family? It could even be your ministry. Are you using it for worship, or has it gotten in the way of your fellowship with the Lord? Remember, anything that keeps you from the Lord is your enemy. You must cut it off at once and allow the Lord to reign alone.

What are some areas in your life that need less attention in order to better serve the Lord?

Will you be sensitive to the Spirit of God and look for opportunities to serve the people in the streets?

Seek the Lord as you read and study Philippians 2:1-11.

Make This Your Prayer Today

Teach me to die, oh Lord
as the prophets of old
Teach me to die daily
by putting others ahead of myself
not just so I can suffer
but so that I can glorify your name
Teach me to walk humbly
Please give me wisdom and discernment Lord
Allow me to share the good news today
Make me bold, urgent, and compassionate
In the name of Jesus I pray,

Amen.

Jan Overstreet

"Devil, I'm going to sting you!"

"For you have died, and your life is hidden with Christ in God."

Colossians 3:3

THE LOCAL STREETS
PART I

"When you are harvesting your crops and forget to bring in a bundle of grain from your field, don't go back to get it. Leave it for the foreigners, orphans, and widows. Then the LORD *your God will bless you in all you do."*

Deuteronomy 24:19

The Lord tells us not to be selfish with our crops. He pleads with us to share the abundance that he's given. We must go through our local streets and share what the Lord has given to us. There are foreigners, orphans, and widows who may not be as well-off as we are. They may not know of the goodness of God. Let us show them who He is by the way we give. This is the ministry that all believers must take part in. All are not called to stand behind a pulpit or lead the congregation in song, but all are called to minister to the orphans and widows.

We must not mistake missions for ministry or vice versa.

John Piper says, "Missions exists because worship doesn't."[49] We should only use the word "missions" when we are talking about people; groups who have never heard of the Gospel. Ministry on the other hand refers strictly with serving others. The word ministry itself means "to serve" or "to serve as a slave." We are called to do both ministry and missions. We are called to the local and foreign streets.

MINISTRY TO THE ORPHANS

"Religion that is pure and undefiled before God, the Father, is this: to visit orphans and widows in their affliction, and to keep oneself unstained from the world."

James 1:27

Who will care for them if we don't? How will they ever know they are loved? How will they know that they have a Heavenly Father who jealously desires them?[50] Let us tell them that, "He is a father to the fatherless."[51] Let us display the same love and affection that our Heavenly Father has shown us.

When I was seventeen, I answered the call on my life to preach the Gospel. I traveled around for two years preaching whenever and wherever the Lord gave me an opportunity. At the age of nineteen, I took my first position at a church full time. I admit that I had no clue what I was doing. All I knew was that I loved the Lord, and I was insufficient to do the work that He had called me to accomplish. I would go to the steps of the Church almost every day and pray that God would send people my way to teach and pour into. Three kids would often skateboard past me as I sat on the steps and prayed. They didn't look like your typical Church-going type but I began to show them the love of Christ. They really didn't know how to respond. Either they had never seen the love of Christ lived out in their life, or they had been too deceived to realize Christ's love in the past. It took me a little while to understand that God was answering my prayer in a way I didn't expect. I was waiting on the nicely groomed Church kids who I've seen in the Church my whole life, but God was sending people my way who have never stepped through a Church door. He was giving me a heart for kids, whose parents didn't take them to Church. They didn't know how to act or speak in a worship service. They lived in the world, acted like the world, and spoke like the world. After I was meeting with God on the steps one day the kids came by. I offered them some water and told them that Jesus loved them. I began to explain what Jesus did for them and they responded to the gospel message. They repented and turned away from living their own way. Within a period of three months, we had seventeen more skateboarders come to know Christ because of the witness of those kids. Many of these kids had parents who loved them, but their parents were not raising them in the fear and admonition of the Lord. They had earthly parents but were spiritual orphans. Although in this passage, James is referring to an orphan in the physical sense; it wouldn't be too far-fetched to look at it in a spiritual sense. God has called us to minister to the physical and spiritual orphan.

There were around 163 million orphaned children recorded all over the world in 2007. This data reflects the number of children who have lost one or both parents due to any cause.[52] I've seen many ministers of the Gospel adopting children over the last 10 years. Most of my friends in the ministry are adopting children. Not necessarily because they can't have children of their own, but because they understand the importance that God puts on taking care of orphans. Many Church members are following the example of their pastors, as they should.

Children, what are you doing to help take care of the orphans? They may sit across the lunchroom table from you at school. Will you love as Christ loves them? Will you take up for them when they are picked on? Will you tell them that God loves and cares for them?

Adults, what are you doing to take care of these children? Will you clothe them, if they need clothes? Will you feed them, if they are hungry? Will you adopt them, if they need a home?

Seek the Lord as you read and study Ephesians 1.

Make This Your Prayer Today

Lord give me a heart for the orphan child
Show me what You want me to do

Teach me to love them as You love them
Show me Lord when You want me to take action
Teach me what to say
Please give me wisdom and discernment Lord
Allow me to share the Good News today
Make me bold, urgent, and compassionate
In the name of Jesus I pray,

Amen

Matthew and Tara Fraser with Mary Alice

Adopted from Taiwan, 2012.

"He predestined us for adoption as sons through Jesus
Christ, according to the purpose of His will."

Ephesians 1:5

SPEAKING LIFE
PART I

"Watch over your heart with all diligence, For from it flow the springs of life."

Proverbs 4:23

SPEAKING LIFE INTO THE DISCOURAGED CHRISTIAN

The discouraged Christian almost always goes astray. He will think badly of himself or someone else until sin creeps in. The discouraged Christian finds a friend in the slothful man. He seeks the company of the world instead of the Lord. Worship services are a bore to him. He will ramble through the songs and sleep through the message. His eyes are open, but his heart is closed. He has lost his appetite for spiritual things. What has happened? He used to be so joyful. He used to long to hear the words of God. Maybe his personal worship is lacking. It could be that he grew weary of doing good.[53] His

Sunday school class could have discouraged him in some way. He may even be upset because some of his disciples are living like the devil and he feels like he has failed. Whatever the reason, he need's words of life. He needs to hear that God loves him and that Christ loves him enough to have died for him. "Depression is a body, soul, and spirit problem that requires a balanced body, soul, and spirit answer."[54] As we write God's word on our hearts, we are supposed to hold them close, so they will not escape until we need them. They are a spring of life that flows from our hearts to the discouraged and thirsty Christian who has neglected God's well. God gives us a charge to speak words of encouragement to the discouraged Christian. We rejoice as we watch the countenence of his face rise. The discouraged Gideon was hiding from the world until the Lord said, "Get up, you mighty man of God!"[55] That was all he needed to hear and he was restored. We need to remind people of how God sees them as we fight off the chains of the defeated spirit. A lot of times we focus on the way we see ourselves and not on the way that God sees us. This will lead to sin if we are not careful. Let us always remember that sin is not ours for it was laid upon Christ's head.

Let us also not forget to encourage our leaders in the Church. The evil one knows, if he can discourage the shepherds, the sheep will scatter. Even Moses needed help as he held up his staff and interceded on Israel's behalf.[56] Sometimes pastors can be some of the most discouraged people. It is good for us to remember to share what the Lord is teaching us with our leaders. This will show them that their labor is not in vain. Galatians 6:6 says, "One who is taught the word must share all good things with the one who teaches." I am often encouraged by young men and women set apart for the Gospel. Thomas Smyly, 15 years old, encourages me often with words of wisdom that was only received from God himself. Joey Luker, at the ripe age of 16, shows me how to truly display the characteristics of a peacemaker. Another 16 year old, Mariah Walker, walks unwavering in her faith. She is not blown about when trials come her way but she is constant in her meetings with the Lord. I could go on and on naming these great witnesses for the Lord, but my point is this: God uses the sheep to encourage the shepherd. So speak up. Share the great truths of the Scripture with them as they share it with you.

Who can you encourage today?

Seek the Lord as you read and study Judges 6.

Make This Your Prayer Today

Lord speak through me I pray
I pray my words would be an outpour of your heart
May I bring encouraging words to the discouraged
And words of life to the dead man
Please give me wisdom and discernment Lord
Allow me to share the good news today
Make me bold, urgent, and compassionate
In the name of Jesus I pray

Amen

"Let each of us please his neighbor for his good, to build him up."

Romans 15:2

THE FOREIGN STREETS
PART I

"Therefore let us go to Him outside the camp."

Hebrews 13:13

We must "have bold, unflinching, lion-like hearts, loving Christ first, and His truth next, and Christ and His truth more than all the world."[57] At times during the Roman Empire when they killed ten believers, one hundred others came forward and said, "Kill me, too." They killed so many Christians during that time the emperors said, "Let's try to save face. Don't kill so many—the place is getting too bloody." I often hear stories of the Chinese Christians who are praying for the American Church. Their prayer is not one that we would expect. They are praying that we would understand what it means to suffer for Christ. They understand first hand that suffering increases one's faith and prove one's love. God's calling often leads us away from our own camp. We learn a small part of who the Lord is in our place of comfort. He bids us to go to the streets and often to the foreign streets. He doesn't promise comfort, safety, or even a place to lay our head but he does assure us of persecution. "Indeed all who desire to live a godly *will be* persecuted."[58] No matter if this persecution takes place in the local or foreign streets, it will take place. If we are not seeing opposition from time to time, we may be in opposition of the Lord. We must learn to cancel hobbies, forsake television, and put away the iPads and magazines. Not that any of these things are bad by themselves, but we must be able to leave them at the drop of a hat if the Lord calls us to do so. We must love God's calling more than we love our toys. We've played enough; people are dying in the streets in need of the Great Physician. He did not heal us so we can grow fat, lazy, and satisfied by our own pleasures. He healed us so we can be useful. Just as He has called **all** Christians to minister in the local streets He has called *all* Christians to the mission field.

> "...you will receive power when the Holy Spirit has come upon you, and you will be my witnesses in Jerusalem and in all Judea and Samaria, and to the end of the earth."
>
> *Acts 1:8*

God told Adam and Eve in the beginning to be fruitful and multiply, fill the earth and subdue it.[59] God desires all people across the globe to sing His praises. Yes, this does mean that we are all called to go. Yes, I know there are few who cannot physically go. These few people should make it their purpose to be diligent in prayer and financial support for those who are going. If this is the only thing they can do to advance the Gospel to the ends of the earth, they must not take it lightly. Everyone else needs to understand that God has called us all to go. He calls some for a few weeks, some for a few months, and others for years. I will never forget the day my professor, Dr. Doug Wilson, said, "Everyone who does not have an active passport is out of the will of God." This statement rocked my worldview. It took a while before I truly began to believe it myself. As I searched the Scriptures, from beginning to end, I too began to agree with him. If we are physically able then we should go from time to time to advance the kingdom. If we are not going, then we should be teaching others to go.

Do you have a heart for the mission field? Will you say as Isaiah said, "Here I am! Send me."[60] "Go into all the world and proclaim the gospel to the whole creation."[61] "Declare His glory among the nations, his marvelous works among all the peoples!"[62]

Seek the Lord as you read and study Isaiah 6.

Make This Your Prayer Today

God, I want to go where you lead me
I don't want anything or anyone to hold me back

Your fame is much too important
Show me how you want me to serve You
Teach me where I should go
Prepare me for your cause
Please give me wisdom and discernment Lord
Allow me to share the good news today
Make me bold, urgent, and compassionate
In the name of Jesus I pray,

Amen.

"Then I said, "Here I am! Send me."

Isaiah 6:8

ALL FISH NEED A SAVIOR

"Follow me, and I will make you become fishers of men."

I will never forget the excitement I had as a kid, going out to the rich soil to look for worms. I would grab my hoe and dig away. The ultimate goal was to find the worm that would look most appetizing, so I could catch some fish. I would dig for hours and fill my bucket up with all kinds of worms. Fat worms, skinny worms, long worms, or even chopped in half worms that did not receive mercy when my blade entered the ground. There are many ways to bait a hook, but my dad taught me to make sure that I had the worm on good, so when the fish nibbled, he would also have to take the hook. I found the perfect fishing spot and threw my line out and waited. If we are to be fishers of men, we must dig and spend hours searching out the great truths of Scripture. Find those great pearls that will no doubt bring repentance to the lost man.[63] Study, study, and study some more, so when the nibbling comes, he will be hooked. God uses various types of methods, methods to call men to himself but some things do not change. The fish is drawn to the hook by the worm and the man is drawn to Salvation by God alone. "No man can come to me," said our Lord, "except the Father, which hath sent me draw him"[64], but God does use us as a witness and proclaimer of the goodness of Salvation. We must be sure to understand that fishing is not just a hobby or something to do in our spare time. We fish for a living. This is our mission. This is our calling. We must become professional fisherman. Well, many of you may say, "I am too scared. What will I say? What do I do?" Dig, dig, and dig so you will not fear anymore. Do you not know that "Faith comes from hearing and hearing through the word of God"[65], His words will fuel your conversations. Yes, some of the fish will be slimy and unattractive but the Lord loves them just as He loves you. Yes, some of the fish may have a foul odor, and may not be your ideal fish, but they all are in need of a savior. Who are we to say which fish is ideal? Does God not make the weak strong, the poor rich, and the sick well? Does He not make the mute sing, the crippled run, and the blind see?

> *"Therefore, if anyone cleanses himself from what is dishonorable, he will be a vessel for honorable use, set apart as holy, useful to the master of the house, ready for every good work."*
>
> *2 Timothy 2:21*

He grabs us where we are and makes us like He is. He is strong where we are weak. In our weakness, He has an opportunity to display His strength. I grew up having to take speech classes because I could not say certain words properly. Now the Lord has me teaching hundreds of students His Word every week. I could never take credit for that, but I can rejoice in what the Lord is doing. I grew up hating to read, but last night I couldn't sleep because I was so excited about getting up and reading about God. One thing is for certain; when Jesus enters your house there will be changes. Those changes will prove your salvation. So let us not doubt our Savior when he tells us where to cast out the line. We do not know the plans that the Lord has for that fish. All we know is that all fish need a Savior.

Are you doing the work that needs to be done before you cast out your line? The passage above says that we must first cleanse ourselves if we are to be useful. The term "cleanse" stresses a cleaning from the inside out. When the Spirit of God enters our temple, His light shines out our darkness. We will see areas that need restoration. We can quench the Spirit and allow that stuff to remain or we can allow God to work. He will take our hand and help us clean house; filthy pile by filthy pile until we are useful again.

Seek the Lord as you read and study John 21.

Make This Your Prayer Today

Lord show me areas in my life that need to be removed

Give me strength to allow you cleanse those areas
I do not want them to remain
I want to be useful for your good works
Help me to be diligent in my study of you
Teach me your words
Write your truths on my heart
Make me a fisher of men
Do not let me show partiality
Please give me wisdom and discernment Lord
Allow me to share the good news today
Make me bold, urgent, and compassionate
In the name of Jesus I pray,

Amen.

"He said to them, "Cast the net on the right side of the boat, and you will find some." So they cast it, and now they were not able to haul it in, because of the quantity of fish."

John 21:6

LIGHT UP THE STREETS

"The people dwelling in darkness have seen a great light, and for those dwelling in the region and shadow of death, on them a light has dawned."

Matthew 4:16

How do we appear as a light in the midst of a crooked and perverse generation?[66] It is not very hard for a believer to shine in the midst of great darkness if he holds close the Words of Light. Light is so undeniably different from darkness. Men are in darkness by birth and remain in darkness through sin. Paul said, "at one time you were darkness, but now you are light in the Lord. Walk as children of light"[67]. God separated the darkness from the light so that darkness and light have no communion; they have nothing in common.[68] Sons of light do not have fellowship with deeds, doctrines, or deceits of darkness neither can darkness bear the fruits of light.[69]

    I remember God putting a desire in my heart to memorize large portions of the Scripture. I spent hours daily, writing His words to my heart and soul. I was so consumed with His words; all I could do was meditate of them. I did not want to do anything, but learn as many truths of God as possible. Without even knowing it, His Word began to consume everything I did and even the way I looked. One day I was walking across the campus at the University of Mobile, quoting Scripture quietly to myself. A man mowing grass saw me and stopped mowing completely. He waited till I got close enough and he asked, "What is different about you?" I'd never met this man before in my life. I just simply responded, "Jesus is good" and then we began to talk about Him. The Lord was gracious to me that day. He allowed me to shine, despite who I am, a sinner in the arms of the Savior.

God is different. We cannot make Him into clay to worship, nor can we display Him on a self. He is not a lowercase g-god but He is the only true God. His kingdom is not of this world and he is considered an outsider or a stranger. We are also called to be a stranger to this world.

"Beloved, I urge you as aliens and strangers"

1 Peter 2:11

We must not, and cannot be a citizen where Jesus is an alien. Jesus said, "My kingdom is not of this world"[70]. The moment of conversion our citizenship is moved from this physical world to His spiritual kingdom. Though still roam this earth, we no longer have a place to lay our head.

Christian, do not get comfortable, for that is the worst thing you can do. No soldier gets entangled in civilian pursuits, since his aim is to please the one who enlisted him.[71] You have been enlisted. You have been called out. "Awake, O sleeper, and arise from the dead, and Christ will shine on you."[72] You have not been called to sleep; but to awaken the dead. Get off the pew. You have not been called to a life of ease, but to a life of suffering.[73] You must learn to pray on your knees. Get up and preach the Word. Tell your families. Tell your friends. Tell your enemies. The Lord is coming. Repent! Repent! You are not alone in your service. Be the light in the streets. Shine so bright that the people will not be able to sleep. Warn them that their estate is in danger of the fire. Drag them out of the streets to the great wedding.[74] Tell them the Groom is on His way. We must get ready.[75]

Where is your home?

Are you content with God alone?

Seek the Lord as you read and study Acts 6, 7.

Make This Your Prayer Today

Lord this is not my home
I pray that I will not become to attached to things that will fade
Give me a yearning only for the everlasting
I want to stand out for your glory
Wake me up when I get worn out or drift away a bit
Help me remember all your words that I study
Please give me wisdom and discernment Lord

Allow me to share the good news today
Make me bold, urgent, and compassionate
In the name of Jesus I pray,

Amen.

"For it is you who light my lamp; the Lord *my God*
lightens my darkness."

Psalm 18:28

THE LOCAL STREETS
PART II

"Honor widows who are truly widows."

1 Timothy 5:3

MINISTRY TO THE WIDOWS

When I think of my wife or mother being left alone, it breaks my heart. God saw that it wasn't good for man to be alone so He created woman. This implies that it is not good for mankind to be alone.[76] It was God's plan that man and woman would leave their parents to be joined together in marriage.[77] As a husband and father, I cannot imagine leaving my wife or children without knowing that they will be taken care of. This is my role as a husband and father. If the Lord calls me home before my wife and children, I want to know that they are going to be taken care of.

There are specific qualifications for widows in 1 Timothy that need to be followed. Is there anyone in your family who is widowed? "If any believing woman has relatives who are widows, let her care for them. Let the church not be burdened, so that it may care for those who are truly widows."[78] We must first tend to our own widows and not let the Church be burdened.

> "Having a reputation for good works: if she has brought up children, has shown hospitality, has washed the feet of the saints, has cared for the afflicted, and has devoted herself to every good work."

> 1 Timothy 5:10

There are widows out there who have no one to look after them. They have honored God with their life, so we should honor them by serving them. Let us cut their grass, rake their leaves, and trim their hedges. Let us sit with them when they mourn. Let us share with them words of encouragement to lift their countenance. If we do this surely the Lord will say, *"For when I was hungry and you gave me something to eat, I was thirsty and you gave me something to drink, I was a stranger and you invited me in, I needed clothes and you clothed me, I was sick and you looked after me"*[79]

MINISTRY UNSTAINED
FROM THE WORLD

"…keep oneself unstained from the world."[80]

The only blood that should be on our hands is the blood of Christ. It is his perfect blood that frees us from the bondage of sin. When people see the Church, they should see a pure and undefiled body of Christ. Not because of our own merit, but because we are stained in the blood of our Savior. If we forsake the Lord for any manner of time we allow the world to spill its stain on us. People will notice and will say like Nietzsche, "You will have to look more redeemed, if I am to believe in your Redeemer". We cannot be stained with Christ and the world for "no one can serve two masters, for either he will hate the one and love the other, or he will be devoted to the one and despise the other."[81] So let us take care of the orphans and widows who are in distress. Let us stay above reproach so that all might see and give glory to our Father in heaven.[82]

Seek the Lord as you read and study 1 Timothy 5.

Make This Your Prayer Today

Lord give me a heart for the widow
Show me what you want me to do
Teach me to love them as you love them
Show me Lord when you want me to take action

Teach me what to say
Help me stay unstained from this world
May others see me and give glory to you
Please give me wisdom and discernment Lord
Allow me to share the good news today
Make me bold, urgent, and compassionate
In the name of Jesus I pray,

Amen.

"For when I was hungry and you gave me something to eat, I was thirsty and you gave me something to drink, I was a stranger and you invited me in, I needed clothes and you clothed me, I was sick and you looked after me, I was in prison and you came to visit me."

Matthew 25:35–36

THE FOREIGN STREETS
PART II

*"And everyone who has left houses or brothers or sisters
or father or mother or children or lands, for my name's
sake, will receive a hundredfold and will inherit
eternal life."*

Matthew 19:29

Worship of the intimate God is our reason for existence.
"The impulse to worship is universal. If there is a race or
tribe anywhere in the world who does not worship, it has
not been discovered."[83] Until worship becomes a completely
personal love experience between God and the lost tribe, we
must continue to go to the ends of the earth. God desires to
make worshipers out of rebels. God's chosen plan is for the
redeemed to spread the good news all across this globe. The
call of God is not for a special few but for everyone. "For many
are called but few are chosen."[84] The chosen ones are the ones

who have entered into a relationship with Jesus Christ. We have been saved and called to a holy calling, not because of our works but because of his own purpose and grace, which he gave us in Christ Jesus before the ages began.[85]

GOING WITH WRONG MOTIVES

Many people go for travel experience, or to get their passport stamped. They post their photos and videos everywhere so others can say, "Look at that young missionary taking care of those little African babies, they are so holy." A. W. Tozer said, "For my part, I am fed up, thoroughly fed up to the teeth, with these wonder boys who go places and come home and entertain you for an offering, and tell you where they have been. O brother, put a *donkey* in a boxcar in St. Louis and send him to Omaha, and when he gets there, he's still a *donkey*."[86]

What about the Gospel? What about the advancement of the Gospel? "How then will they call on him, in whom they have not believed? And how are they to believe in him of whom they have never heard? And how are they to hear without someone preaching?"[87] Will you answer this holy calling? Will you go?

Nowadays, we give more monies towards companies and organizations that water down the Gospel (if they preach at all) in order to be tolerant. We give to them only because they give us shoes or other fashions that let the world know of our giving. These may be great companies but do not think for a moment that we are advancing the Gospel by our fashion sense. The church's motives must move beyond the easing of physical hunger and pain. It must not be rooted with a spirit of humanitarianism, but with the Spirit of God. Our motives for advancing the Gospel to the ends of the earth need to be pure, if we are going to be fruitful.

On a trip to Guatemala, I met with a 12 year old kid named Johnny who my wife and I are sponsoring. I asked him if he needed any school supplies or clothes etc... and he responded, "Just food." I was deeply broken over his situation as I walked him back to his 10 ft. by 10 ft. house that is in the middle of a landfill. Of course, I am doing everything in my power to make sure Johnny doesn't have to go to sleep hungry. It is very important to take care of one's physical needs, if possible, but our goal should be to introduce them to the Great Physician. Two years earlier, I was able to introduce Jonni to Christ and now he is faithfully leading others to Jesus even though he is just a kid.

Will you answer this holy calling? Will you go? I believe it will only take one trip and you will understand God's heart. Let Him show you how He deeply cares for all peoples.

Seek the Lord as you read and study Isaiah 6.

Make This Your Prayer Today

God, I want to go where you lead me
I don't want anything or anyone to hold me back
Your fame is much too important
Show me how you want me to serve you

Show me how deeply you care for all the peoples in the foreign streets
Teach me where I should go
Prepare me for your cause
Please give me wisdom and discernment Lord
Allow me to share the good news today
Make me bold, urgent, and compassionate
In the name of Jesus I pray,

Amen.

Johnny

"Just food"

"And he went out, not knowing where he was going."
Hebrews 11:8

SOUL-WINNING

"Repent and be baptized every one of you in the name of Jesus Christ for the forgiveness of your sins, and you will receive the gift of the Holy Spirit."

Acts 2:38

How much do we value the souls of our neighbors? "The soul's greatness is demonstrated by the great price that Christ paid for it with his precious blood, making it an heir of glory."[88] God thought that our soul was of such great value that He paid His Son's life for it. Although the soul is the most valuable thing in the world, we often pay such little attention. "Soul-winning is the chief business of the Christian minister; indeed, it should be the main pursuit of every true believer."[89] Our goal should not be the growth of a clan but the increase of the kingdom. We cannot consider stealing other members from Churches already established as soul-winning.[90]

BE BOLD

*"For God gave us a spirit not of fear but of
power and love and self-control."*[91]

God forgive us for not being bold enough at times. I sat down
with three kids the other day. We talked about things that
were not worth discussing. The Lord spoke into my heart
and said, "What are you here for? No reason to waste time.
So I shared the Gospel with those kids. Two of the three
were already Christians. The other kid asked Jesus to forgive
him and save him that very moment. God has enabled us
with a spirit of boldness and not timidity.[92] How often do
we continue to talk about things that do not matter when
God wants us to speak of Him? Ragan Ferguson, one of
my students, shared Jesus with Nicholas Cage while he
was shooting a movie in Mobile, Alabama. Picture this—a
fifteen-year-old girl walking up to her favorite actor while
he was working out and asking him where he thought he
was going after he died. Nicholas's response broke her heart.
He had no clue. She continued to share with him because
she knew what she had was so much more than a picture or
an autograph. Ragan explained later, "Nicholas Cage is one
of the most famous and richest men on the planet, but what
good is it to gain the whole world but lose your soul?"[93] The
next day Danny Glover approached her at the pool. She had
no clue who he was. She just thought he was a nice old man.
I wonder what Danny Glover was thinking. He may have

thought here is this sweet little girl. She looked at him and said, "Sir, who is Jesus to you?" He was taken aback and said, "Whoa, baby girl, I'm a Muslim!" Her words were as sharp as a double-edged sword from God Almighty. He left the conversation as fast as he could.

BE URGENT

*"Repent, for the kingdom of the Lord is at hand."*94

I woke up this morning to another upsetting text message. Another kid committed suicide. He hugged his grandmother and with his last words he said, "Nobody loves me". I visit the school lunchrooms every Wednesday to evangelize and would often sit with this kid. Today, I've tried my best to recall our conversations about Jesus. I really do not remember sharing Christ with him. I have no clue if he had a relationship with Jesus or not. This is another reminder to me that we are called to urgency. We are not guaranteed tomorrow. Our life is like a vapor that appears for a little while then it vanishes.95 We must tell our family, friends, and enemies that Jesus is the only way to have salvation.96

If we knew that the Lord was coming back tomorrow for His people, how would that change our sense of urgency? Would we rush to our friend's house and urge them to repent and seek the Lord? Of course we would.

BE COMPASSIONATE

"When He went ashore He saw a great crowd, and He had compassion on them and healed their sick."[97]

If we come in arrogance, or in a prideful spirit, the people in the streets will not listen. Jesus looked at the crowds and he had compassion for them. His inward parts battled within himself over the state of his lost sheep. He led out of a state of compassion and love. If we want to see people come to know Jesus we must really care. If we don't care then they won't care to listen.

Seek the Lord as you read and study Matthew 3:1-12

Make This Your Prayer Today

*Lord, make me bold to proclaim your Good
News with all urgency
I want to see people with the same
compassion that You do
Use me to lead the lost sheep to You
Please give me wisdom and discernment Lord
Allow me to share the good news today
Make me bold, urgent, and compassionate
In the name of Jesus I pray,*

Amen.

"Behold, I am coming soon, bringing my recompense with me, to repay each one for what he has done."

Revelation 22:12

SPEAKING LIFE
PART II

"The tombs also were opened. And many bodies… who had fallen asleep were raised"

Matthew 27:52

SPEAKING LIFE INTO THE DEAD MAN

Jesus' glorious death brought the dead man to life. Our death to the things of this world should bring others to life spiritually as well. If people are not coming to Christ by the way that we live, then we must speak up. Jesus said, *"Lazarus, come out"*[98] and the dead man woke up. God's word has power and authority to wake up the deadest of dead. People are starving for God's word even though they may not know it yet. I was discouraged when I began youth ministry because many churches expected games but not the word. Their ministries were there to entertain, but not to seek and save the lost. But the Lord gave me a hunger to have a different youth group; one that I wouldn't be ashamed to present to the Lord on the Day of Judgment. I will never forget the first night I taught them God's Word. They were so intrigued and hungry for His Words. Those fifteen students turned into seventy-five within four months. I didn't have flashy games, and I didn't even bribe them with food, but all I had were words of life. I watched that group continue to grow, and be sent out over the next three years. Now my family is blessed to be in Thomasville, Alabama. God has led us to employ the same practices in Thomasville. We watched as God turned thirty students to hundreds within a couple years and are still overwhelmed every day at how God has made them hungry to hear his Word. There is no secret or grand strategy that one must have to see people wake up from their sin. You must only speak words of life to them and allow the spirit of God to do the rest. We will be held accountable for the things that we teach those God puts in our charge. If we teach our disciples to stay and to play, that is what they will teach their disciples; but if we teach them to go and pray, they will teach others to do the same. When you speak, do not speak as a dead man yourselves, for why would a dead man listen to a dead man? He has nothing to offer.

Many televangelists we see today know a lot about God, but their lack of depth tells us a different story. Their cold boring faces reminds us of those in the grave, and not of those that are alive. There is a big difference between knowing about God and knowing God. Also, we must make sure we know what we are saying when we say it. The passionate fool will lead others astray. As my professor would often tell us, "let us not be cold scholars nor passionate fools; but let us press on to be passionate scholars." Let us speak as men and women of unction who proclaim life by the authority of Jesus Christ. As we walk the streets, the Holy Spirit walks with us. He is the One who wakes them up, but it is our privilege to speak on his behalf.

Has the Holy Spirit reminded you of someone who needs words of life today?

Will you begin to speak life and not death into people?

Seek the Lord as you read and study James 3.

Make This Your Prayer Today

Lord speak through me I pray
I pray my words would be an outpour of your heart
May I bring encouraging words to the discouraged
And words of life to the dead man
Please give me wisdom and discernment Lord
Allow me to share the good news today
Make me bold, urgent, and compassionate
In the name of Jesus I pray,

Amen.

"Death and life are in the power of the tongue, and those who love it will eat its fruits."

Proverbs 18:21

THE PURSUIT
PART II

"That I may know Him"

Philippians 3:10

"How tragic that we in this dark day have had our seeking done for us by our teachers. Everything is made to center upon the initial act of 'accepting' Christ (a term, incidentally, which is not found in the Bible) and we are not expected thereafter to crave any further revelation of God to our souls."[99] We have allowed our church services to be tainted with this logic; we have found Him, so no need to seek Him. Many of our services are dull or boring because of the lack of pursuit of God by our pastors, deacons, and members. Yet, every time I've met with the Lord, I've never been bored or put to sleep; but overjoyed with the sweetness of his fellowship. We could say like C. H. Spurgeon said, "There are too many dead pastors preaching too many dead sermons to too many dead people,"[100] but when it comes down to it, we cannot take the speck out of our brother's eye if we first don't remove the log from our own.[101] If we want to see people awakened, our worship to be genuine, and our church to be in the streets, we must first pursue God ourselves in worship. Christian, do you really want to know Him? Do you seek for Him like one seeking treasure? Do you pursue Him like a drowning man pursues air? Our constant pursuit of the Lord will spill over to our corporate worship, which will fill the streets with God's goodness. We will never reach the people outside the church walls if we are not pursuing the Father. Our desire to see other people come to know Jesus grows only if we are seeking him first.

> *"…they recognized that they had been with Jesus."*

> *Acts 4:13*

"There's something different about you." "Why are you always happy?" "How do you treat people with love even when they mock you?" "What do you have that I don't have?" We should long to hear these questions. Our prayer should be that when others see us, they will have to say, "Those people have been with Jesus. Surely they walk with the Lord." Spending much time with Jesus in spirit and truth must take place if people are to notice Jesus in us. Personal contact with Jesus alters everything.[102]

Our personal pursuit of the Lord will open the door to share the good news of Jesus. I will never forget walking down the streets of Ukraine as people followed us to church. One little street sweeper cornered my mentor, and before he could even say a word, she pleaded with him to tell her about Jesus. Yes, we looked different because we were Americans, but we acted different because we were Christians.

Jesus tells us about a man who found a treasure in a field; and with joy, he sold everything he had to buy that field.[103] The daily pursuit of the Lord is the constant tearing off of our fleshly and earthly desires to sit at the feet of the most treasured. Every minute we spend with God is a minute enriched with new life and strength from God. Jesus should be our priceless jewel that we have no problem giving up all that we have to possess.

Is He what you *treasure most*?

Do you have the willingness to turn off the TV, iPod, iPhone, and all other distractions to pursue the God who wants to be found?

As we meet with Jesus, people will notice that we have been with him; it is impossible for us to hide Him. This reminds me of a story told about little Chris. He asked Jesus into his heart, one day. He had many questions and began to ask his grandpa about God. He asked, "How big is God, Grandpa?" Grandpa began to explain the bigness of God to Chris. He told of how God created the universe and the galaxies. Chris was overwhelmed and asked him "Grandpa, if God is so big and He is in my heart, shouldn't He be poking out somewhere?"

"Come, let us go up to the mountain of the LORD*"*

Isaiah 2:3

Do not stop pursuing God personally. Go to the place that He calls. Stand firm on the rock, like Moses, until He reveals himself.[104] Be still and listen. Plead to hear His voice calling, "Come up higher, my child." When it's time, let us step-off the mountain of God and share what he has taught us in the streets.

Seek the Lord as you read and study Psalm 63.

Make This Your Prayer Today

Jesus, forgive me for my lack of pursuit in the past
I want to want You
I long to have a deeper longing for You
Only your water can satisfy my thirst
Take away my distractions
Let me sit at Your feet
Make your word my delight
My heart, my deeds, my words
May others see that they are of You
Oh that I would know You more
Oh that they would know You
Please give me wisdom and discernment Lord
Allow me to share the good news today
Make me bold, urgent, and compassionate
In the name of Jesus, I pray,

Amen.

Ukrainian Street Sweeper

"Tell Me About Jesus."

"Let us know; let us press on to know the LORD; *his going out is sure as the dawn; he will come to us as the showers, as the spring rains that water the earth."*
Hosea 6:3

DEPENDENT ON HIS SPIRIT
PART II

*"I know how to be brought low, and I know how to
abound. In any and every circumstance, I have learned
the secret of facing plenty and hunger, abundance and
need."*

Philippians 4:12

POOR IN SPIRIT—
MIGHTY IN THE STREETS

Everywhere we turn we see the verse, "I can do all things
through him who strengthens me."[105] Sports teams carry this
verse as a banner. Schools make it their motto. Thousands of
shirts preach it to the streets everyday but I wonder if those
who carry this Scripture truly understand its meaning. I do
believe this verse is taken out of context more than any other
verse of Scripture. Paul tells the Philippians, in the verse
before, that he has learned to be content with God alone.

He is not saying that he can hit a homerun further than any other because Jesus gives him strength. He is not even saying that we can run an extra 10 miles because the Holy Spirit is within us. Though this may be true, it is not the Apostle Paul's meaning. These thoughts are often rooted in pride and not humility. Paul is saying that he has learned a secret. King David also writes of this secret in Psalm 73, "My flesh and my heart may fail, but God is the strength of my heart and my portion forever."[106] God is all we need. Whatever circumstance we may find ourselves in

We have no heavy loads to carry. We have no reason to sweat. Yes, our enemies are before us. Yes, there are giants on every side, but who can stand before our Lord? Our downfall can only be found in self-reliance. If we choose to fight or carry loads by our own means then we will fail. If we choose to use our own words they will lack authority and power. "No matter what changes God has wrought in you, never rely upon them, build only on a person, the Lord Jesus Christ, and on the Spirit He gives. All our vows and resolutions end in denial because we have no power to carry them out."[107] It is God who awakens the dead man. It is God who makes himself known to the sinner. It is good for us to remember, *"…neither he who plants nor he who waters is anything, but only God who gives the growth."*[108] This is no reason for us to be upset but it gives us reason to rejoice. God told the Israelites, *"Do not be afraid and do not be dismayed at this great horde, for the battle is not yours but God's."*[109] We have no need to fight this battle alone. For the God of all creation is on our side. He will make us mighty in the streets. Let us remember to humble ourselves in the presence of God and he will exalt us.[110] We must be poor in our spirit to make much of his Spirit. Let us say again to the Lord, "I have nothing! But I am Yours!"

Seek the Lord as you read and study Acts 2:41-47.

Make This Your Prayer Today

It was You Lord that saved me
It was You Lord that changed me
It is You Lord that saves alone
I have nothing! But I am Yours!
Please give me wisdom and discernment Lord
Allow me to share the good news today
Make me bold, urgent, and compassionate
In the name of Jesus I pray,

Amen.

"...let your adorning be the hidden person of the heart with the imperishable beauty of a gentle and quiet spirit, which in God's sight is very precious."

1 Peter 3:4

DO YOU LOVE ME?

"I remember the devotion of your youth, your love as a bride, how you followed me in the wilderness, in a land not sown."

Jeremiah 2:2

You are not in love with me now, but I remember the time when you were,[111] I remember... your love as a bride, how you followed me... I have this against you, that you have abandoned the love you had at first. Remember therefore from where you have fallen; repent, and do the works you did at first.[112]

Christian, how deep is your love towards Jesus? Does it grow stronger every day or is he speaking the words above directly to your heart? Do you not know that "he yearns jealously over the spirit that he has made to dwell in us"?[113] Have you allowed sin to creep in and steal your love? Maybe you used to feel like the chosen, but now you feel like the frozen. Perhaps the most severe charge that can be said about many Christians today is that we are not sufficiently in love with the Lord. Praise God, there is grace for us but let us remember the greatest command from our Lord, "You shall love the Lord your God with all your heart, and with all your soul, and with all your mind."[114]

> *"We love because He first loved us."*
>
> *1 John 4:19*

He was betrayed, arrested, spit on, beaten, mocked, crucified with nails in His hands and feet to glorify the Father and show His love for us. Do you understand? "He wrestled with justice, so that you could rest; He cried and mourned, so that you could laugh and rejoice; He was betrayed, so that you could go free; He was arrested, so that you might escape; He was condemned, that you might be declared innocent, and He was killed, so that you could live. He wore a crown of thorns, so that you could wear a crown of glory; and He was nailed to the cross with His arms wide open, to show how freely He gives everything He has. All this He did, simply because He loves us."[115] He loves us for who we are and values us more than any created worlds or galaxies. But do we love him? We can sing, "I love you, Lord" all day long but if we don't back it up by our actions our words are in vain. We must prove our love. Let me say it again: Christian, let us prove our love.

The apostle Paul was devoted to a person not to a cause.[116] He was undeniably Jesus Christ's, he sought nothing else and he lived for no one else, "For I determined to know nothing among you, except Jesus Christ, and Him crucified."[117] No amount of fame, money, success, or blessings can compare to the "view of the surpassing value of knowing Christ Jesus my Lord."[118] He tells us that our love must be sincere.[119]

It is not hard for me to love my wife. Every day that I spend with her, I fall more and more deeply in love with her. I often think there is no way that I could love this girl any more than I do, but then I spend more time with her and I'm proven wrong yet again. I must prove my love to her by the things I do. If I only tell her I love her, but do not act out this love, I am not being the husband I am called to be. Do not get me wrong; I have a deep desire to prove my love for her because I truly care for her. It is never out of a sense of duty, but out of a longing to display my love. The same should be true with our relationship with God. We prove our love for Him because we truly love Hm. Love must be backed up with action or it is not pure love.

"Anyone who does not love does not know God, because God is love. In this the love of God was made manifest among us, that God sent his only Son into the world, so that we might live through him."[120]

How do fall in love with Him?

"We can love without worshiping but we cannot worship without loving."[121] The more we sit at the Lord's feet, the more we understand what it means to sincerely love. He alone displays true unadulterated love. There is so much more to God than just love, but there is no more to the word love, but just God. For example, God defines love but He also defines grace, peace, and justice. These words find their meaning and purpose in God, but God cannot be defined by these words alone. So we must spend some time with the only one who knows what it correctly means to love. Christian, do you love Him? God proved His love by sending His only son into the world to die on a cross. What are you doing to prove your love?

Seek the Lord as you read and study I John 4.

Make This Your Prayer Today

Father teach me how to love
Show me what this word means
I love You Lord
Give me opportunities to prove it
But I need Your strength
For apart from You I am nothing
But I am Yours
Please give me wisdom and discernment Lord
Allow me to share the good news today
Make me bold, urgent, and compassionate
In the name of Jesus I pray,

Amen

"Who shall separate us from the love of Christ?"

Romans 8:35

– 104 –

BROKENNESS
PART I

"And immediately the rooster crowed a second time. And Peter remembered how Jesus had said to him, "Before the rooster crows twice, you will deny me three times." And he broke down and wept."

Mark 14:72

BROKEN OVER PERSONAL SIN

I often catch my little girl doing something that she is not supposed to. Most of the time she breaks down and cries before I even speak a word. She cries not because she is sorrowful for her sin, but because she got caught and she knows discipline is to come. Peter *broke down and wept* not because he got caught but because he was truly broken. He understood at that moment what Isaiah meant when he said, *"Woe is me, for I am ruined! Because I am a man of unclean lips, And I live among a people of unclean lips; For my eyes have seen the King, the* LORD *of hosts.*"[122] When the living Christ draws near to our lives, we are quickly overwhelmed by our sinfulness and must respond in brokenness. True brokenness must take place if we are going to be healed. As our relationship with the Lord grows, we will be broken more and more over time. This is nothing to dread but something to seek. Jesus said, *"Blessed are those who mourn, for they shall be comforted."*[123] The comfort that the Lord is talking about is the forgiveness of our sins. He desires us to be in right fellowship with Him at all times. "If there is anything in us that does not worship God, then there is nothing in us that worships God perfectly."[124] No worship is wholly pleasing to God as long as we have something displeasing in us. He doesn't ask for part of our life but he asks for all of it. We will never be comforted until we are sorrowful and broken over our sins. We will not be the church God has called us to be, until we quit asking for forgiveness with a weak faith. We must stop throwing up uncaring prayers and expect the Lord to forgive us. Repentance doesn't take place, unless we are truly sorrowful for our sins. This will not take place if we think that our sins are not that bad. Some people "give fair names to foul sins; call them what you will, they will smell no sweeter. No matter how excellent our words may be, if our heart is not conscious of the hell-deservingness of sin, we cannot expect to find forgiveness."[125] We must understand that if sin rules in us, God's life in us will be killed: if God rules in us, sin in us will be killed.[126] It may be that we know our sin better than we know our Savior. Let that horrible thought break our hearts. For brokenness is the beginning of hatred towards sin. Spurgeon says, "You have learned to hate sin; but you have also learned how that is not yours—it was laid upon Christ's head." So yes, we are called to mourn over sin but let us remember, *"Weeping may tarry for the night, but joy comes with the morning"[127]* or I guess we could say joy comes from the mourning.

BROKEN OVER THE STRUGGLING CHRISTIAN

"Bring them back! Lord, please bring them back! They have denied you, Lord. They have returned to their old ways. They were showing great promise. They were doing so good. I saw your light on their face. Their eyes spoke of your grace, but now they won't even look me in the eyes. Lord, please bring them back!"

"We who are strong have an obligation to bear with the failings of the weak, and not to please ourselves. Let each of us please his neighbor for his good, to build him up."[128]

Every Christian I've ever poured my life into has gone through times of struggle. It is very important for us not to give up on them but to intercede for them. There are a few things that will take place as they run from the Lord. They will run from anything spiritual including us. Yes, this does hurt but our plea should not be "Lord, return them to us", but it should be "Lord, may they return to You". When they return to the Lord they will also return to us. If we plea that our relationship be mended without first seeking that they repent, that shows us that we have self-seeking motives. If we do this, we are not seeking first the Kingdom of God, but we are seeking a friendship that will not last. Let us be broken over the back-sliding Christians. Let us pray that they would return to the Lord. Let us be there for them and in love lead them back. "Let him know that whoever brings back a sinner from his wandering will save his soul from death and will cover a multitude of sins."[129]

Seek the Lord as you read and study Romans 6.

Make This Your Prayer Today

I pray that I would learn to hate sin as you do
Lord forgive me for all of my sins
Help me lead others back to you Lord
Please give me wisdom and discernment Lord
Allow me to share the good news today
Make me bold, urgent, and compassionate
In the name of Jesus I pray,

Amen.

"Who is able to stand before the LORD, *this holy God?"*

1 Samuel 6:20

BROKENNESS
PART II

"When he saw the crowds, he had compassion for them, because they were harassed and helpless, like sheep without a shepherd."

Matthew 9:36

BROKEN OVER THE LOST MAN

During a Spirit-anointed time of worship a man returned to the Lord after years of wandering and failure. Those who were present will no doubt remember his prayer for some time. "While praying, he broke into tears and was unable to finish, for the Lord had revealed to him something of the lostness of men."[130] Surely one who is broken over the lost man has encountered the Lord Almighty. This burden is borne out of a pursuit for the Lord's heart. The closer our fellowship with the Lord gets, the more compassion we feel towards the lost man. The word compassion in this sense means to have one's bowels yearn with inward affection; it is a yearning of the inmost nature with pity, or sympathy. When Jesus sees the lost sheep he feels deep inward affection and pity or to put in other words: He cares for them.

"The harvest is past, the summer is ended, and we are not saved."[131]

After Jesus had compassion on the crowds He told His disciples, "The harvest is plentiful, but the laborers are few;"[132] He had to tell them because they were not seeing the people as He did. One would think after spending so much time with Jesus that the disciples would have the same compassion for the lost but they didn't. He had to show them that there was much work to be done. Jeremiah paints a tragic picture of what happens to the lost men and women when Jesus returns. He shows us from the viewpoint of the lost man (the wheat). The wheat says to the other wheat "The harvest is past, the summer is ended, and we are not saved." They did not listen. They did not seek the Lord. They chose the hang with the weeds instead of God's people. The only thing that is left for them is the fire. Let this break our heart today.

The fear of the Lord gripped my entire being when I realized that I was not saved. I knew that if I were to die I would go to hell. I was broken and truly sorry for my sins. I see kids with this same fear every now and then. They weep because they are broken over their sins. They know without some miracle, they are going to be totally separated from God in hell. So they plead, "Save me, Lord! Save Me!" If the parents of these kids would more fully understand the condition that their kids are in; they would weep as well. If they had a healthy fear of the Lord; they may also realize that they need to repent. We must tell them, "There are no exits in hell! We are here on earth for such a small time. You must repent! Compel your family to repent also, while there is still time." It's God's will that not one sinner would die, but rather that all should return, repent, and live.[133]

Seek the Lord as you read and study Luke 15.

Make This Your Prayer Today

Lord I want to care
I pray that I would be broken over the lost man
May I wake up with an urgency to proclaim Your truth
Please give me wisdom and discernment
Allow me to share the good news today
Make me bold, urgent, and compassionate
In the name of Jesus I pray,

Amen.

"I will seek the lost, and I will bring back the strayed, and I will bind up the injured, and I will strengthen the weak, and the fat and the strong I will destroy. I will feed them in justice."[134]

Boldness

And now, Lord, look upon their threats and grant to your servants to continue to speak your word with all boldness, while you stretch out your hand to heal, and signs and wonders are performed through the name of your holy servant Jesus." And when they had prayed, the place in which they were gathered together was shaken, and they were all filled with the Holy Spirit and continued to speak the word of God with boldness.

Acts 4:29-31

Even though I spent a few paragraphs on boldness already I must continue on this topic because of its extreme importance. Pray Bold—Speak Bold—Act Bold.

PRAYING BOLDLY

"And when they had prayed, the place in which they were gathered together was shaken"

When we pray we must pray in confidence in His Word. "We will never receive if we ask with an end in view; if we ask, not out of our poverty but out of our lust."[135] James says, "But let him ask in faith, with no doubting, for the one who doubt is like a wave of the sea that is driven and tossed by the wind. For that person must not suppose that he will receive anything from the Lord; he is a double-minded man, unstable in all his ways."[136] We must approach the throne room of God boldly with our prayers not because of our own merits but because of the blood of Jesus.[137] Praying boldly is not a sign of irreverence but it shows that we trust in the Lord and what he says.

SPEAKING BOLDLY

"Lord, look upon their threats and grant to your servants to continue to speak your word with all boldness."

The early church constantly prayed for boldness. Jesus spoke boldly even though they sought to kill him.[138] Are their souls more important to you than your life? We know that we have a place set aside for us in heaven but the people in the streets are choosing the here and now instead of the eternal. Speaking boldly should come from an outpouring of God's Spirit and not in a spirit of pride. Some people are loud but that doesn't make them anymore godly than a bird. Many Churches try to be bold by using their Church signs. They put up their clever words and rhymes thinking that will attract the people. Who are we to speak our foolish words that will fade away instead of the speaking the Word of God? Only the Spirit can penetrate the heart in such a way to cause instant change. Our words must be fueled by His words for it is His words that we cannot contain. It is out of an outpouring of His Word and His Spirit with us in a state of humility that we speak boldly on His behalf.

ACTING BOLDLY

"You stretch out Your hand to heal, and signs and wonders are performed through the name of your holy servant Jesus."[139]

Five minutes before Elijah appeared on the scene, no one had any idea that he was in the offing; five minutes after he came in the power of the Spirit, a nation knew "there was a man sent from God."[140] Sometimes God tells us to do bold things for His purpose. A few years ago I was with a group of my friends sharing the Gospel in some village schools in China. Missionaries are not officially allowed in China but we knew we must go. The first couple of days went very well and we were able to share the Gospel with thousands of kids. But the cops began to bug our rooms and follow us through the streets. We had to hide in certain buildings to have conversations about Jesus. The village that we were in has never seen Americans in person, so we couldn't hide very well. Especially since we were twice their size. As we were finishing up in one school, the cops came by and kicked us out of the school. God was not through with us yet. We prayed and God gave us a fearless spirit. So we went to one more school that was five blocks away from the one we just got kicked out of. We were able to preach the Gospel to thousands more students before the cops found us.

Have you been praying boldly? Have you been speaking without fear? Have you been living in a spirit of timidity?

Seek the Lord as you read and study Joshua 1.

Make This Your Prayer Today

God I want to
Pray boldly
Speak boldly
Act boldly
Only You can give me a fearless spirit
I am nothing without You Lord
I am wholly Yours
Please give me wisdom and discernment Lord
Allow me to share the good news today
Make me bold, urgent, and compassionate
In the name of Jesus I pray,

Amen.

School in a Village in China

"We must obey God rather than men."

Acts 5:39

THE SILENT CHRISTIAN

"If I say, 'I will not mention Him, or speak any more in His name,' there is in my heart as it were a burning fire shut up in my bones, and I am weary with holding it in, and I cannot."

Jeremiah 20:9

There's something wrong; if the Christian man refuses to talk. Some believe that we should keep our mouths shut at all times, and let our actions speak for themselves, but this is foolish. God gave us a mouth for a reason and that is to use it. I struggle with understanding the logic of refusing to talk. If this is the case, then we should also refuse to walk, to hear, to look, and even go as far as to refuse to breath. Then we might as well return to the grave from which we were raised. God has given us a mouth to express all the wonders that generate inside our being. If His word penetrates your heart then you will proclaim it in the streets. Jeremiah says, "I am weary of holding it in, I cannot"[141]. God speaks fire into us that we cannot contain. If God is close to our heart, we will talk about Him! Some people say, "I'm just worshiping God in my heart, I have no need to sing praises aloud"; but maybe they are making excuses because they haven't generated enough spiritual heat to get their mouth open![142] "There are some things they have never seen and can't describe—that's their trouble. There are some places they have never been—so they are on unfamiliar ground. That's their trouble."[143] We have been charged by God Himself to proclaim the good news. If we remain silent one might believe that the good news isn't good anymore.

As a child, my hero was Mike Reader (our local weatherman). I wanted to grow up to be just like him. I thought he had the greatest job. He was able to chase tornados and be on TV. In my eyes he was a superhero. On 7th grade, our class took a trip to the TV station. I was overwhelmed with the opportunity to meet him. I was saddened when I found out he was not there. As I was leaving the building a man pulled up into the parking lot and all the students flocked to his car. As I fought through the crowd I realized that it was Mike Reader. As he shook my hand he looked me in the eyes and said, "Hey!" I just sat back in awe. I thought to myself, "I will never wash this hand!" From that moment on I couldn't speak of anything else. All day long I told everyone that I met Mike Reader, the man who predicts the weather!!! Even though some of their faces told me that they could care less, I still opened my mouth. Why? Because it was great news. We have every reason to open our mouth. We have met the God of the Universe, the one who not only can predict the weather, but can tell the weather what to do. He said, "Be still"[144] and wind and seas obeyed him. I would like to see Mike Reader try that. The Lord took our hand and pulled us out of the domain of darkness;[145] this should be reason enough to proclaim His goodness from the rooftops. If one has an encounter with the Most High, one cannot wash Him off and one doesn't even want to. He must sit back in awe of His majesty. How can that man remain silent? Even when others mock him, will he not still speak of the Lord's goodness? The Gospel means, "Good News" for a reason. It has not lost its goodness. Church we still have Good News. Let us not be silent while people are dying who don't know Jesus as their Lord and Savior. Sit at the feet of Jesus today. Let Him remind you of His goodness. To quote the old Christmas carol, *"Go, tell it on the mountain, over the hills and everywhere;"*

Seek the Lord as you read and study Exodus 4:10-17.

Make This Your Prayer Today

Teach me when to speak and when to remain silent Lord
You have given me great news please don't ever let sin creep in and steal my joy
May my words be seasoned with salt
May I proclaim Your goodness to the streets
Please give me wisdom and discernment Lord
Allow me to share the good news today

Make me bold, urgent, and compassionate
In the name of Jesus I pray,

Amen.

"The LORD *said to him, "Who has made man's mouth? Or who makes him mute or deaf, or seeing or blind? Is it not I, the* LORD*?"*

Exodus 4:11

HYPOCRISY, HYPOCRISY, HYPOCRISY

"A good name is to be chosen rather than great riches"

Proverbs 22:1a

"Hypocrisy! I will never go to Church there because of all the hypocrites." How often do we hear these statements? The first response that comes to my mind is found in Romans where Paul says, "no one is good"[146]. Yet, the Holy Spirit reminds me that Christians are called to be above reproach. We should never get caught in the sin of hypocrisy. We are called to be holy, pure, and selfless. "Jesus did not condemn sinners; He condemned hypocrites."[147] "People today are not tired of preaching but tired of our preaching."[148] They are tired of people who say one thing but yet do another. We cannot remain hypocrites and at the same time find holiness. If the horrible sin of hypocrisy is in the Church it must be removed. We must plead to the Father right now:

Lord, protect our reputation
Keep us above reproach
Don't let us stand in the way of people coming to you
Bless our name so that we can bless yours

If a good name is better than great riches, then a bad name must be worse than the poorest of the poor. When a man is caught in hypocrisy most likely all he would want to do is escape; escape from the sight of all men; escape from all of his duties. Run, run, run would be the plea of his heart. He is disgraced and ashamed. He knows that he has let his family, friends, and neighbors down. He should have pleaded, *"Lord, Protect my reputation"*, but instead, he put his faith in himself and tried to fight his own battles. He lied and lied again to cover his faults. His name used to be his glory, but now it is his shame.

If we are going to be the church in the streets we must give God everything, including our name. The day we called upon the Lord for salvation was the day we stopped carrying our name and began carrying his. Only he knows how to properly carry his name. I love the word "Christian" because it literally means, "little Christs". It is a constant reminder that I am a small part of a larger picture. Tozer says, "You and I are in little, (our sins excepted) what God is in large."

"Indeed all who desire to live for the Lord will be persecuted"

Do not be deceived by praying for God's protection over our reputation does not mean we will be free from persecution. Persecution comes to all the godly.[149] If the evil ones can't get us to sin, they will send their wolves to lie. They will circle us and throw their darts from every side, so we must be prepared and well armed. But consider it a great joy, for just as they persecuted the perfect and spotless Lamb, they will persecute us. Even though Stephen was above reproach he was still attacked and martyred. Job did not sin but his reputation was ripped into pieces. These men lived out the passage that says, "Do not fear those who kill the body but cannot kill the soul. Rather fear him who can destroy both soul and body in hell."[150]

Years ago, I was going through the streets of Launceston, Tasmania sharing the good news of Jesus along with Callum Reece, a new believer in Christ. We walked up to a middle-aged Australian man and began to speak with him. I will never forget his response as soon as I mentioned that we were Christians. To my surprise, he began to curse and spit at us. The hatred in that man's eyes and heart overwhelmed me. We walked a bit further and sat on a bench. We watched some women who called themselves witches. They were dressed in all black and had a sense of coldness in their eyes. As we would meet to pray on Thursday nights safely within the church walls, the witches would meet in the park to pray (to the Evil One) for the downfall of Christians. Do not be fooled. Everyone who doesn't call upon the name of the Lord are His enemies. They will try their best to shame the name of Jesus or anyone who carries that name. Be on guard. Stand firm. Carry His name and allow Him to protect yours.

Will you give Him your name today?

Seek the Lord as you read and study Genesis 32:22-32

Make This Your Prayer Today

Lord, protect my reputation
Keep me above reproach
Don't let me stand in the way of people coming to You
Bless my name so that I can bless Yours
Show me how to rejoice in the midst of persecution
May others look at me and give glory to You
Please give me wisdom and discernment Lord
Allow me to share the good news today
Make me bold, urgent, and compassionate
In the name of Jesus I pray,

Amen.

Young Callum in the streets of Launceston, Tasmania

"Daniel answered and said: 'Blessed be the name of God forever and ever, to whom belong wisdom and might'."

Daniel 2:20

THE GREAT PEARL CALLED WISDOM

"...they stood in awe of the king, because they perceived that the wisdom of God was in him to do justice."

1 Kings 3:28

King Solomon found this great pearl called wisdom. Throughout his whole life he spoke of this great treasure. He did not gain it from experience even though we often learn from our experiences and even our mistakes. I seek council from a good friend of mine named Gary Cockerham. He was one of the first men that my wife and I met as we arrived at our new home in Thomasville, Alabama. Even though he is 40 years older than me, we are still great friends. He had an accident about a year ago where he fell out of a tree house that he was building for his grandchildren. He laid on the ground for some time thinking that he was about to die. He finally crawled back to the house and got some help. A couple of months after the accident, he was talking with some of the students and myself as he said, "Even if my circumstances don't get any better, I still have every reason to praise the Lord". I don't think I will ever forget that statement. Every time I seek wisdom from Mr. Gary, he always replies, "You want wisdom from a man who almost broke his neck trying to climb up a tree?" And I always respond, "No Sir, I want wisdom from the man that crawled back to the house and knew never to try that again." Yes, Mr. Gary grew in wisdom that day but God is so gracious that we don't have to fall out of a tree to gain wisdom. All we have to do is ask, as Solomon asked. *"If any of you lacks wisdom, let him ask God, who gives generously to all without reproach, and it will be given him."*[151]

SPEAKING WISELY

"The godly offer good counsel; they teach right from wrong."

Psalm 37:30

The child of God should always choose his words wisely. For *"…on the day of judgment people will give account for every careless word they speak."*[152] We should always watch our words. Our conversations should only be filled with life bringing subjects. If we cannot please the Lord with our conversation then we should be quiet. Proverbs says, *"Whoever keeps his mouth and his tongue keeps himself out of trouble."*[153] A few chapters before Solomon said, "Even a fool who keeps silent is considered wise; when he closes his lips, he is deemed intelligent."[154] I loved and hated my Biblical Greek classes in college. I love the insight into the Scriptures but I hated reading aloud a language that was foreign to me. I dreaded going to class because I was scared my professor was going to call on me. Sadly, I have to admit skipping a few times, not because I didn't do the work, but because I just didn't want to read aloud. As long as I never opened my mouth in the class; people would continue to think I knew what I was doing, but the moment I opened my mouth, it was evident that I had no clue how to read Greek. This passage by no means implies that we should never speak but it does; however, imply that we should not speak of foolish things. Our speech should be above reproach. We should strive to speak as Stephen, one of the seven chosen to serve, "…they could not withstand the wisdom and the Spirit with which he was speaking."[155] He was not a king or even one of the twelve apostles but yet he had great wisdom. This type of wisdom can only be gained by sitting at the feet of our Lord. "Jesus never uttered opinions; He never guessed; He knew, and He knows. His words are not as Solomon's are, the sum of sound wisdom or the results of keen observation. He spoke out of the fullness of his Godhead, and His words are very Truth itself."[156]

ACTING WISELY

It is one thing to speak as a wise man but quite another to act as one. Solomon could talk the talk, but often fell prey to the sins he preached against. We must pray that the wisdom that the Lord gives would not fall on deaf ears.

"Even when the fool walks along the road, his sense is lacking and he demonstrates to everyone that he is a fool."[157]

A wise man walks with integrity staying above reproach. He exceeds everyone's expectations. He is a perfectionist because his heavenly Father is perfect. He doesn't seek wisdom from this world but he is "other-worldly". He thinks different than the people of this world. He acts different than the people in the streets. They flock to him because they see he has something that they don't. They are tired of seeing fools so they are intrigued to watch this man of wisdom. He visits the same stream of wisdom every day. He is the perfect apprentice. He takes great joy in learning from his master—the wisest of all. He pays special attention to the master's ways; he makes them his own. He knows that every act of his life is or can be as truly sacred as prayer or baptism or the Lord's Supper. He holds close the Sacred Writings, "…whether you eat or drink, or whatever you do, do all to the glory of God."[158] He knows that reverence and boasting cannot be found on the same platform. He tells all who will listen that the fear of the Lord is the beginning of wisdom.[159]

Have you spoken and acted wisely this week? Have you visited with the Wisest of all? It's only through Him that we can be truly wise.

Seek the Lord as you read and study Proverbs 1.

Make This Your Prayer Today

Lord I pray that I would seek after wisdom
like a man searches for great riches
Teach me to fear You so I can be wise
Give me wisdom Lord not for my Glory
But so I may lead many others to You
Allow me to share the good news today
Make me bold, urgent, and compassionate
In the name of Jesus I pray,

Amen.

"If any of you lacks wisdom, let him ask God, who gives generously to all without reproach, and it will be given him."

James 1:5

ENLARGE MY TERRITORY

"Oh, that you would bless me and enlarge my territory!
Let your hand be with me, and keep me from harm so
that I will be free from pain."

1 Chronicles 4:10

There is a wall that needs to be torn down. This wall separates us from the outside world. It contains elements of pride, fear, race, and other unwritten excuses that continue to pile up between the lost sheep and our testimony. Our borders must advance. We can no longer remain here quiet and hungry. God is calling us to a higher place. Our view of the Lord is way too small it must expand. There are new mysteries on the horizon, more graces with every step. One wolf says, "What will you say?" The sheep reply, "The Lord will give us the words." Another wolf cries out, "They will make fun of you." The sheep respond, "It will be our great joy to suffer for Christ's sake." All the wolves in one voice say, "We will devour you if you go." The sheep reply, "For us to live, is

Christ and to die is gain"[160]. The Lord does not want us to remain in the familiar. We must be on the move spiritually and often physically.

"These have no root"

Luke 8:13

The Holy Spirit is leading us to grow upward and downward at the same time. He desires us to be firmly planted by the Great River, but He is also calling us to go into the dark wilderness. Is this possible? Can we remain planted and still go? Not only is this possible but it is the only way. If we uproot and go to the wilderness without the nourishment of the Lord, we will be overcome and devoured. But if we remain like the *tree planted by water, which sends out its roots by the stream*[161], all we can do is expand. This tree *does not cease to bear fruit* and does not have to rely on others for nourishment.

I was overwhelmed by a great tree, which caught my eye as I was going through the Amazon in a canoe. I was amazed at the great tree from a distance; and the closer I got, the more impressed I became. This tree seemed to have no boundaries. Its branches reached well over the river, deep in the dark jungle; it reached as high as the heavens, and still had a firm grip on the earth. The tree wasn't going anywhere; yet it was going everywhere. Thousands of creatures would come, sit, and eat. If the tree could talk, it would say, "Come and eat there is plenty to go around. I am truly fortunate because I get to live by the Great River. I am blessed so let me bless you."

God is calling us to cross the boundaries of the familiar. We can no longer remain content with last year's crop. *"Look, I tell you, lift up your eyes, and see that the fields are white for harvest."*[162] His Spirit is calling us to advance.

For years I relied on what I learned in college. As a college student, I had few responsibilities, so I spent most of my time reading, or studying the Bible. When I was in a position of influence, I taught them everything I knew about God, but after a while I had nothing else to teach. I was empty. I was out. I taught them everything I learned from God during my quiet times and classes. I didn't know it at the time, but I slowly uprooted myself from the river of God, and began to rely on myself, or other preachers for my spiritual food. Because I didn't meet with God daily, I put boundaries and limitations on what the Lord wanted me to do. He was calling me to advance but I didn't hear him. He was calling me to speak up, but I remained silent. He wanted to bless me but I was unaware.

Are you listening to the Lord today? He is calling you to the unfamiliar. Will you go? Are you willing to do something out of your comfort zone if He asks? Do not put up borders in your heart today. Stay firmly planted by the Great River and allow the Lord to build you up and send you out.

Seek the Lord as you read and study Galatians 5.

Make This Your Prayer Today

Lord bless me so I can be a blessing to others
Enlarge my territory
I don't want to stand in the way of what You want to do
Break down any walls that I've allowed to rise up
You are strong where I am weak
Please give me wisdom and discernment Lord
Allow me to share the good news today
Make me bold, urgent, and compassionate
In the name of Jesus I pray,

Amen.

The great tree in Ecuador, 2009

"Remember not the former things, nor consider the things of old. Behold, I am doing a new thing; now it springs forth, do you not perceive it? I will make a way in the wildernessand rivers in the desert."

Isaiah 43:18-19

DISCIPLESHIP
PART I

"Be imitators of me, as I am of Christ."

1 Corinthians 11:1

Jesus poured into the twelve disciples more than He did the crowds. He poured into three, more than the other nine, and even in the midst of the three, He spent more time with one. This is how discipleship works. Jesus could have called fire down from the heavens and made everyone believe, but that wasn't His plan. Discipleship was and still is His plan. The apostle Paul took discipleship to heart better than any other example we have in the Scriptures, apart from Jesus Himself. In 2 Timothy, he pleads with Timothy (his disciple) to continue with discipleship. "You then, my child, be strengthened by the grace that is in Christ Jesus, and what you have heard from me in the presence of many witnesses entrust to faithful men who will be able to teach others also."[163] Teach others, so that they can teach others. If we, as the church, would treasure this passage, and apply it to our lives we would fulfill the Great Commission easily within this generation.

HIS EXAMPLE

"Come, follow me,"[164]

It wasn't an allotted hour or a discipleship class that Jesus used to disciple men. He simply said, "Come, follow me," and they did. They became true imitators of Christ. They spoke, worked, and walked as he did. If Jesus went to town they went to town. Where Jesus stayed, they stayed. Where he went, they went. They learned to live at the feet of Jesus. They desired His fellowship so often that Jesus would have to "slip away"[165] in order to have some one on one time with the father. Discipleship must be more than a program, or it will not be worth a dime. It must be a lifestyle.

DISCIPLESHIP AS A LIFESTYLE

I first learned of discipleship from my seventhth grade history teacher. I remember rushing to get in the front of the lunch line, not so I could eat first, but so I could make sure that I got to sit next to Mr. Tony during lunch. Sometimes, I even skipped eating so I could be sure to get a close seat. The words of encouragement and Scripture that he spoke into my life, as a seventh grader, still have an impact today. If we had a ballgame, I could always look up in the stands and see

Mr. Tony. My youth pastor poured into me during my high school years. God has used him to influence my life more than any other, apart from my family. He would take me with him as he did everyday errands. I watched the way he treated others. I observed him share the Gospel on a daily basis. I was humbled as he treated me as a son even though I already had a dad. He constantly prayed for me and encouraged me in the faith. He would give me opportunities to preach the Gospel home and abroad. He would often say, "You only have to know one more thing about the Lord to disciple someone. Share that one thing with them, so they can share it with someone as well."[166]

1-3-9-27-81-243-729-2187-6561-19683-59049-177147-531441-1594323-4782969-14348907

The numbers are staggering. Most people would never believe that they could reach millions for the Lord but it is true. Even if we just pour into three people for the rest of our life, we could still see millions discipled through those few. Not with a baby-like faith but mature believers in the Lord. "Go therefore and make disciples…"[167]

Seek the Lord as you read and study 2 Kings 2.

Make This Your Prayer Today

Lord give me wisdom and discernment to lead

I need You Lord
I can't lead them in a manner pleasing to You
If I'm not sitting at Your feet
Lord may millions come to know You because
of the work You're doing in and through me
Teach me to act justly, love mercy, and walk humbly
Allow me to share the good news today
Make me bold, urgent, and compassionate
In the name of Jesus I pray,

Amen.

"Paul… To Timothy, my beloved child: Grace, mercy, and peace from God the Father and Christ Jesus our Lord."

2 Timothy 1:1-2

DAY 30

DISCIPLESHIP
PART II

"As soon as he had finished speaking to Saul, the soul of Jonathan was knit to the soul of David, and Jonathan loved him as his own soul."

1 Samuel 18:1

Many people say the greatest joy, apart from accepting Christ, is leading others to Christ. I must disagree. There is an inexpressible joy that comes when the people we disciple begin to lead others to Christ. This joy continues when they disciple others to do the same. Two years after twelve year old Johnny came to know Jesus, I got the opportunity to see him again. He drew a picture on the sand of two cliffs. God was on one side, and man was on the other. His drawing pointed out that sin is in the way of man meeting with God. This was the same sketch that I drew for him on the sand as I lead him to Christ. I stood in amazement as I watched him preach the Gospel to his friends by drawing same exact photo on the sand. I didn't have to remind him of anything. He remembered every single detail. Before I left his village I shared with him the same words as Paul shared with Timothy. "The things which you have heard from me in the presence of many witnesses, entrust these to faithful men who will be able to teach others also."[168]

EASY DISCIPLESHIP

"As the Lord lives, and as you yourself live, I will not leave you."[169]

Even after Elijah asked his disciple Elisha to leave He would not. He said, "I will not leave you." If Elijah really wanted Elisha to leave he could have made him but I believe Elijah wanted Elisha to stay if he wanted to. These types of disciples are such a blessing. I have the great joy of discipling some students with a clinging spirit like Elisha. I was cutting my grass the other day and one of my students saw me in the yard. He got out of his truck and began to weed-eat. I didn't ask him to. I refused his help a couple of times but he wasn't taking no for an answer. He desired to talk with me about the Lord so much that he would work to get some time. We cut the grass, rode to the store, grabbed some food, and talked about Jesus. Some people God will send our way without us even expecting it. If they are hungry for Godly counsel, we must seek the Lord and give it to them. We may look for the well-versed and well-mannered young believer, but God may send us someone who has never stepped foot in a Church building. To be honest, sometimes it's better if they haven't. When God sends people to us to pour into, we must take advantage of the time He gives us. We must make sure that we don't corrupt the time with countless video games or movies etc. There may not be anything wrong with these activities, but don't let it consume the time; for what we teach them, they will teach others. Let us be sure that when they are with us, we allow the Spirit to control our conversations and actions.

TOUGH DISCIPLESHIP

"let him know that whoever brings back a sinner
from his wandering will save his soul from death
and will cover a multitude of sins."[170]

Sometimes, God uses disciples with a clinging spirit to encourage us when other disciples are breaking our hearts. We may love and care for them, but it doesn't mean they will always listen. At times, it seems like they understand everything, but at other times it seems they could care less. During these times, we must fight for them. We should never give up or stop praying for them. Several years ago the Lord allowed me to teach a young student named Garrett. God impressed on my heart to pray for him daily. I spent four out of seven days a week teaching him everything I knew. This lasted a couple of years, until he begin to break away. This "breaking away" period quickly became my least favorite part of discipleship. It broke my heart because I looked at him as a son in the faith. Over time I've realized that it is very important for him to break away on his own. During this breakaway period, disciples learn to discern God's voice from their teacher's. If we are not careful, we will "over-disciple" and they will look to us, instead of looking to the Lord. We must not play the role of the Holy Spirit in their life. They may run from us and even run from the Lord, but that doesn't mean that we should give up on them. We must continue to pray and be there for them if they need counsel. God heard my prayer with Garrett and he came back stronger than ever, full-on for the Lord. There are very few days when he does not encourage me with Scripture or conversation. I am overjoyed when I see what the Lord is doing with him.

Don't give up! Regardless if you are discipling the easy or the tough do not give up on them! Remember that even Jesus's disciples returned to fishing for fish after Jesus left, but God called them back and they were stronger than ever with the power of the Holy Spirit.

Seek the Lord as you read and study 2 Timothy 2–4.

Make This Your Prayer Today

Lord help me be a light to people around me
Give me wisdom to share what You want me to

Give me strength to remain strong
even when it seems others abandon me
Lord bring them back
May they return to You
Give them strength to overcome temptations
Allow me to share the good news today
Make me bold, urgent, and compassionate
In the name of Jesus I pray,

Amen.

Johnny Sharing Christ With A Friend

"Two are better than one, because they have a good
reward for their toil. For if they fall, one will lift up his

fellow. But woe to him who is alone when he falls and has not another to lift him up!"

Ecclesiastes 4:9–10

ENDNOTES

1 James 4:4

2 Philippians 2:15

3 Matthew 5:3

4 Oswald Chambers, *My Utmost For His Highest*, (Uhrichsville, Oh: Barbour Publishing, 1935), May 5th.

5 Psalm 16:2

6 Philippians 1:6

7 Neil T. Anderson

8 John 8:44

9 Revelation 12:9

10 1 John 5:19

11 John 8:32

12 Proverbs 6:6

13   Charles Spurgeon, *The Soul Winner*, (CreateSpace Independent Publishing Platform, 2011).

14   Isaiah 2:13

15   Leonard Ravenhill, *Revival Praying*, (Bethany House Publishers, 2005).

16   Leonard Ravenhill, *Revival Praying*, (Bethany House Publishers, 2005).

17   Leonard Ravenhill, *Revival Praying*, (Bethany House Publishers, 2005), 40.

18   A. W. Tozer, *The Chief End of Man, Sermon #6*, (Toronto, 1962).

19   Charles Spurgeon, *The Soul Winner*, (CreateSpace Independent Publishing Platform, 2011). (some words were changed to fit the right tense)

20   Exodus 23:22

21   1 Kings 19:11-12

22   A. W. Tozer

23   Romans 8:26

24   A.W. Tozer, *The Pursuit of God*, (Camp Hill, Pennsylvania: Wing Spread Publishers, 1982).

25   A.W. Tozer, *The Pursuit of God*, (Camp Hill, Pennsylvania: Wing Spread Publishers, 1982).

26   Half of the sentence taken from Job 5:30a

27   Luke 11:11

28 Charles Spurgeon, *The Soul Winner*, (CreateSpace Independent Publishing Platform, 2011).

29 Leonard Ravenhill, *Revival Praying*, (Bethany House Publishers, 2005), 129.

30 2 Timothy 2:6

31 Proverbs 14:4

32 Charles Spurgeon, *The Soul Winner*, (CreateSpace Independent Publishing Platform, 2011).

33 Philippians 3:8

34 Psalm 46:4

35 Proverbs 17:5

36 Matthew 7:2

37 A.W. Tozer, *The Pursuit of God*, (Camp Hill, Pennsylvania: Wing Spread Publishers, 1982).

38 Matthew 16:24

39 Romans 6:6

40 Philippians 3:8

41 1 Corinthians 15:55

42 Philippians 2:1-11

43 Matthew 11:29 (KJV)

44 Philippians 2:1-11

45 John 3:30

46   Philippians 3:8

47   1 Corinthians 15:31

48   Matthew 5:30

49   John Piper, *Let The Nations Be Glad!*, (OMF Literature Inc.,), 15.

50   James 4:5

51   Psalm 68:5

52   These numbers are based on Orphan Estimates published by the United Nations Children's Fund (UNICEF) in 2009.

53   Galatians 6:9

54   Neil T. Anderson

55   Judges 6

56   Exodus 17:11

57   Charles Spurgeon, *The Soul Winner*, (CreateSpace Independent Publishing Platform, 2011).

58   2 Timothy 3

59   Genesis 1:28

60   Isaiah 6:8

61   Mark 16:15

62   Psalm 96:3

63   Proverbs 20:15

64   John 6:44

65   Hebrews 10:17

66   Philippians 2:15

67   Ephesians 5:8

68   2 Corinthians 6:14

69   Ephesians 5:11

70   John 18:36

71   2 Timothy 2:4

72   Ephesians 5:14

73   Matthew 5:11-12

74   Matthew 22:1-14

75   Matthew 24:44

76   Genesis 2:18

77   Genesis 2:24

78   1 Timothy 5:16

79   Matthew 25:35-36

80   *James 1:27*

81   Matthew 6:24

82   Matthew 5:16

83   A.W. Tozer, *The Pursuit of God*, (Camp Hill, Pennsylvania: Wing Spread Publishers, 1982).

84   Matthew 14:22

85 2 Timothy 1:9

86 I changed the word jackass for the word donkey

87 Romans 10:14 NASB

88 John Bunyan, *The Riches of Bunyan*, (Uhrichsville, Oh: Barbour Publishing, INC., 1973).

89 Charles Spurgeon, *The Soul Winner*, (CreateSpace Independent Publishing Platform, 2011).

90 Charles Spurgeon, *The Soul Winner*, (CreateSpace Independent Publishing Platform, 2011). Thought reworded

91 2 Timothy 1:7

92 2 Timothy 1:7

93 Mark 8:36

94 Matthew 3:2

95 James 4:14

96 John 14:6

97 Matthew 14:14

98 John 11:43

99 A.W. Tozer, *The Pursuit of God*, (Camp Hill, Pennsylvania: Wing Spread Publishers, 1982).

100 Spurgeon Sermons

101 Luke 6:43

102 Oswald Chambers, *My Utmost For His Highest*, (Uhrichsville, Oh: Barbour Publishing, 1935).

103 Matthew 13:44

104 Exodus 33

105 Philippians 4:13

106 Psalm 73:26

107 Oswald Chambers, *My Utmost For His Highest*, (Uhrichsville, Oh: Barbour Publishing, 1935), June 11th.

108 1 Corinthians 3:7

109 2 Chronicles 20:15

110 James 4:10

111 Oswald Chambers, *My Utmost For His Highest*, (Uhrichsville, Oh: Barbour Publishing, 1935).

112 Revelation 2:4-5

113 James 4:5

114 Matthew 22:37

115 John Bunyan, *The Riches of Bunyan*, (Uhrichsville, Oh: Barbour Publishing, INC., 1973).

116 Oswald Chambers, *My Utmost For His Highest*, (Uhrichsville, Oh: Barbour Publishing, 1935).

117 1 Corinthians 2:2

118 Philippians 3:8 NASB

119 Romans 12:9 NIV

120 1 John 4:8-9

121 A.W. Tozer, *The Pursuit of God*, (Camp Hill, Pennsylvania: Wing Spread Publishers, 1982).

122 Isaiah 6:5 NASB

123 Matthew 5:4

124 A.W.Tozer, *The Pursuit of God*, (Camp Hill, Pennsylvania: Wing Spread Publishers, 1982). (Changed tense)

125 Charles Spurgeon, *The Soul Winner*, (CreateSpace Independent Publishing Platform, 2011).

126 Oswald Chambers, *My Utmost For His Highest*, (Uhrichsville, Oh: Barbour Publishing, 1935), (Changed Tense).

127 Psalm 30:5

128 Romans 15:1-2

129 James 5:20

130 Leonard Ravenhill, *Revival Praying*, (Bethany House Publishers, 2005).

131 Jeremiah 8:20

132 Matthew 9:37

133 2 Peter 3:9

134 Ezekiel 34:16

135 Oswald Chambers, *My Utmost For His Highest*, (Uhrichsville, Oh: Barbour Publishing, 1935).

136 James 1:6-8

137 Hebrews 10:19-25

138 John 7:26

139 Acts 4:30

140 Leonard Ravenhill, *Revival Praying*, (Bloomington, Minnesota: Bethany House Publishers, 1962), 21.

141 Jeremiah 20:9

142 A.W. Tozer, *The Pursuit of God*, (Camp Hill, Pennsylvania: Wing Spread Publishers, 1982).

143 A.W. Tozer, *The Pursuit of God*, (Camp Hill, Pennsylvania: Wing Spread Publishers, 1982).

144 Mark 4:39

145 Colossians 1:13

146 Romans 3:10

147 Francis Frangipane

148 Paul Althus via Leonard Ravenhill, *Revival Praying*, (Bloomington, Minnesota: Bethany House Publishers, 1962), 20.

149 Matthew 5:11-12

150 Matthew 10:28

151 James 1:5

152 Matthew 12:36

153 Proverbs 21:23

154 *Proverbs 17:28*

155 Acts 6:10

156 A.W. Tozer, *The Pursuit of God*, (Camp Hill, Pennsylvania: Wing Spread Publishers, 1982).

157 Ecclesiastes 10:3

158 1 Corinthians 10:31

159 Psalm 111:10

160 Philippians 1:21

161 Psalm 1:3

162 John 4:35

163 2 Timothy 2:1-2

164 Matthew 4:19 NIV

165 Luke 5:16

166 Barry Jemison

167 Matthew 28:19a

168 2 Timothy 2:2 NASB

169 2 Kings 2

170 James 5:20

185 67315

09 05 51 02 008 1655 08409